University Success
READING AND WRITING

BEGINNING

Tim McLaughlin

University Success Reading and Writing, Beginning

Copyright © 2020 by Pearson Education, Inc.

All rights reserved.

No part of this publication may be reproduced, stored in a retrieval system, or transmitted in any form or by any means, electronic, mechanical, photocopying, recording, or otherwise, without the prior permission of the publisher.

Pearson Education, 221 River Street, Hoboken, NJ 07030

Staff credits: The people who made up the *University Success* team, representing content development, design, multimedia, project management, publishing, and rights management are Pietro Alongi, Sheila Ameri, Stephanie Callahan, Tracey Cataldo, Dave Dickey, Gina DiLillo, Warren Fischbach, Sarah Henrich, Niki Lee, Agnieszka Leszkiewicz, Amy McCormick, Robert Ruvo, Katarzyna Starzynska-Kosciuszko, Paula Van Ells, and Joseph Vella.

Project management: Debbie Sistino

Instructional Design: Tim McLaughlin

Contributing author and MyEnglishLab author: Christen L. Savage

Contributing editors: Eleanor Kirby Barnes, Linda Butler, Jaimie Scanlon, Leigh Stolle, and Sarah Wales-McGrath

Video development: Christen L. Savage

Video production: ITN Productions

Text composition: EMC Design Ltd

Library of Congress Cataloging-in-Publication Data

A catalog record for the print edition is available from the Library of Congress.

Printed in the United States of America

ISBN-10: 0-13-524592-3

ISBN-13: 978-0-13-524592-7

1 2019

Contents

Welcome to *University Success*

INTRODUCTION

University Success is a five-level academic series designed to equip beginning through transition level English learners with the language skills necessary to succeed in university courses. At the upper levels, the three strands, Reading, Writing, and Oral Communication, are fully aligned across content and skills and provide students with an inspiring collection of extensive authentic content. The series has been developed in cooperation with subject matter experts, all thought leaders in their fields. The upper levels are organized around five distinct content areas—The Human Experience, Money and Commerce, The Science of Nature, Arts and Letters, and Structural Science. By focusing on STEAM topics, *University Success* helps equip students with the critical thinking skills and creative innovation necessary for success in their future careers.

University Success levels from Intermediate to Transition model the type of real-life learning situations that students face when studying for a degree. The lower levels, Beginning and High-Beginning, lay the groundwork and build the support that students need to prepare them for the complexity and challenge of the upper levels.

BUILDING THE FOUNDATION

Beginning students face a daunting challenge as they build the English-language skills needed for academic success. The Beginning and High-Beginning levels support these students by providing the scaffolding to construct a strong linguistic core. The two integrated skills strands (Reading and Writing and Listening and Speaking) include four distinct content areas that link to the content areas of the *University Success* upper levels. This allows students to build a background in basic concepts and vocabulary in these STEAM content areas: Business, Humanities, Structural Science, and Natural Science. These levels fuse high-interest, engaging content with carefully scaffolded tasks to develop the language skills needed for managing complex and conceptually challenging content.

Task types are recycled across content areas to reinforce skills and give students the confidence they need to take on ever-more challenging material. By using Bloom's Taxonomy as a framework, *University Success* strongly emphasizes the learning process. The series's targeted approach to vocabulary instruction includes both academic and high-frequency vocabulary and provides the basic building blocks needed to construct meaningful speech and writing. A variety of level-appropriate input, as well as visuals, organizers, and critical thinking and discussion activities enable students to fully internalize the content and solidify their linguistic foundation.

TWO STRANDS SUPPORT THE PATH TO LEARNER AUTONOMY

The two lower-level strands are fully aligned across content areas and skills, allowing teachers to utilize material from different strands to support learning. The strands are complementary, providing the teacher with aligned content across all four skills to be utilized in an integrated skills classroom. This allows students to build a solid background in basic concepts and vocabulary in each of the four content areas.

BEGINNING LEVEL
CEFR A1   **GSE** 22–32

READING AND WRITING

Architecture

Genetics
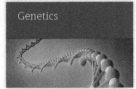

Business and Technology

Psychology

LISTENING AND SPEAKING

Architecture

Genetics

Business and Technology

Psychology

SKILLS

- Identify the main idea
- Understand compare and contrast
- Express likes and preferences
- Write basic descriptions
- Write basic directions

SKILLS

- Understand the gist
- Identify compare and contrast signposts
- Express likes and preferences
- Describe people, places, and things
- Give basic instructions

HIGH-BEGINNING LEVEL
CEFR A2–A2+   **GSE** 33–42

READING AND WRITING

Money and E-Commerce

Cultural Anthropology

Civil Engineering

Sustainable Agriculture

LISTENING AND SPEAKING

Money and E-Commerce

Cultural Anthropology

Civil Engineering

Sustainable Agriculture

SKILLS

- Preview and predict
- Scan for details
- Recognize narratives
- Follow steps in a process
- Write a simple story
- Describe visuals

SKILLS

- Predict
- Listen for details
- Identify events in a narrative
- Understand steps in a process
- Tell a story
- Describe objects

BUILDING THE FOUNDATION FOR *UNIVERSITY SUCCESS*

Two integrated-skills strands with explicit skill development tied to specific learning outcomes establish the foundation for higher-level academic success.

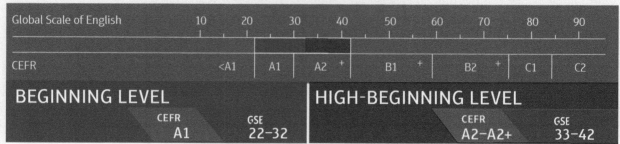

Global Scale of English	10	20	30	40	50	60	70	80	90
CEFR		<A1	A1	A2 +	B1 +	B2 +	C1	C2	

BEGINNING LEVEL
CEFR A1 **GSE 22–32**

HIGH-BEGINNING LEVEL
CEFR A2–A2+ **GSE 33–42**

BEGINNING LEVEL	HIGH-BEGINNING LEVEL
The Beginning level gives students the fundamental building blocks and confidence to take on academic challenges.	The High-Beginning level builds the support that prepares students for the rigor and challenges of the upper levels and beyond.

INTENSIVE SKILL PRACTICE

Intensive skill practice tied to learning objectives informed by the Global Scale of English	Intensive skill practice tied to learning objectives informed by the Global Scale of English

ACADEMIC HIGH-INTEREST CONTENT

■ Academic content linked to STEAM disciplines provides a bridge to the upper levels. ■ Introducing each unit is a video featuring an overview of the academic area. ■ High-interest topics and a variety of genres increase motivation. ■ Two chapters within each content unit include recycled tasks and vocabulary and give students a solid background in basic concepts.	■ Academic content linked to STEAM disciplines provides a bridge to the upper levels. ■ Introducing each unit is a video featuring a university professor, which gives students an academic perspective. ■ High-interest topics and a variety of genres increase motivation. ■ Two chapters within each content unit include recycled tasks and vocabulary and give students a solid background in academic concepts.

SCAFFOLDED APPROACH

■ Chapters are heavily scaffolded with multiple guided exercises that follow Bloom's Taxonomy as a framework. ■ Prediction and skill comprehension tasks accompany each reading and listening. ■ Step-by-step application of all productive skills is practiced throughout each chapter. ■ Readings and listenings are "chunked" and include accompanying visuals. ■ Extensive integration of graphic organizers is included.	■ Chapters are carefully scaffolded with multiple guided exercises that follow Bloom's Taxonomy as a framework. ■ Practical application of all productive skills is integrated in every chapter. ■ Readings and listenings are "chunked," with skill and comprehension tasks integrated throughout. ■ Extensive use of graphic organizers aids in note-taking.

EXPLICIT VOCABULARY INSTRUCTION

A targeted approach to vocabulary including • contextualized previews with pronunciation practice • reviews in the Student Book and in MyEnglishLab • collaborative tasks • vocabulary tips • a vocabulary building and expansion section • an end-of-chapter vocabulary checklist	A targeted approach to vocabulary including • vocabulary tasks pre- and post-reading and listening • vocabulary tips and glossing of receptive vocabulary • a vocabulary strategy section in every chapter • online reviews with pronunciation practice

GRAMMAR FOR WRITING / SPEAKING

A dedicated grammar presentation with controlled practice tasks in the Student Book and in MyEnglishLab provide scaffolding for the writing and speaking tasks.	■ A dedicated grammar presentation prepares students for authentic writing and speaking tasks. ■ Grammar practices in the Student Book and in MyEnglishLab move from controlled to practical application.

SOFT SKILLS

Task-based strategies linked to chapter topics focus on academic success, life skills, and college readiness.	Task-based strategies linked to chapter topics focus on academic success, life skills, and college readiness.

PUTTING STUDENTS ON THE PATH TO *UNIVERSITY SUCCESS*

Intensive skill development and extended application—tied to specific learning outcomes—provide the scaffolding English language learners need to become confident and successful in a university setting.

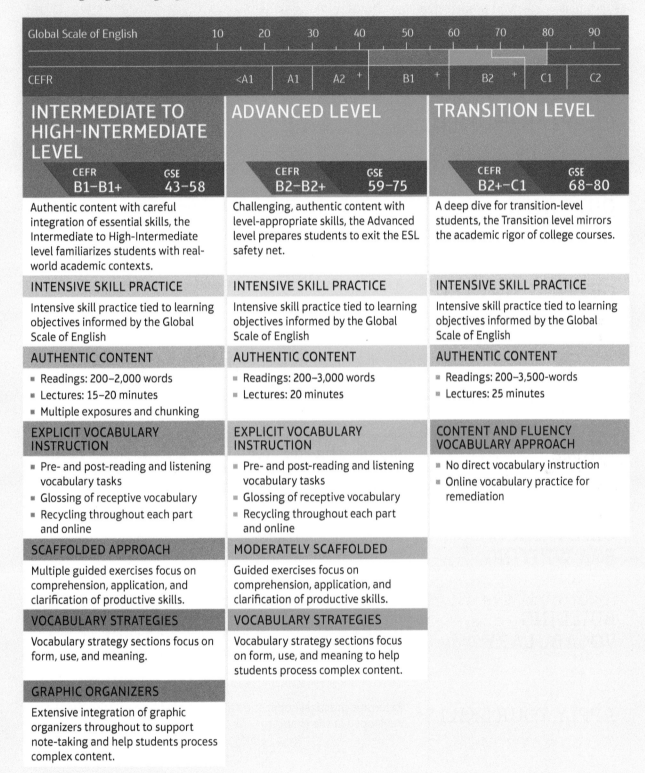

Global Scale of English	10	20	30	40	50	60	70	80	90
CEFR		<A1	A1	A2 +	B1 +	B2 +	C1	C2	

INTERMEDIATE TO HIGH-INTERMEDIATE LEVEL

CEFR	GSE
B1–B1+	43–58

Authentic content with careful integration of essential skills, the Intermediate to High-Intermediate level familiarizes students with real-world academic contexts.

INTENSIVE SKILL PRACTICE

Intensive skill practice tied to learning objectives informed by the Global Scale of English

AUTHENTIC CONTENT

- Readings: 200–2,000 words
- Lectures: 15–20 minutes
- Multiple exposures and chunking

EXPLICIT VOCABULARY INSTRUCTION

- Pre- and post-reading and listening vocabulary tasks
- Glossing of receptive vocabulary
- Recycling throughout each part and online

SCAFFOLDED APPROACH

Multiple guided exercises focus on comprehension, application, and clarification of productive skills.

VOCABULARY STRATEGIES

Vocabulary strategy sections focus on form, use, and meaning.

GRAPHIC ORGANIZERS

Extensive integration of graphic organizers throughout to support note-taking and help students process complex content.

ADVANCED LEVEL

CEFR	GSE
B2–B2+	59–75

Challenging, authentic content with level-appropriate skills, the Advanced level prepares students to exit the ESL safety net.

INTENSIVE SKILL PRACTICE

Intensive skill practice tied to learning objectives informed by the Global Scale of English

AUTHENTIC CONTENT

- Readings: 200–3,000 words
- Lectures: 20 minutes

EXPLICIT VOCABULARY INSTRUCTION

- Pre- and post-reading and listening vocabulary tasks
- Glossing of receptive vocabulary
- Recycling throughout each part and online

MODERATELY SCAFFOLDED

Guided exercises focus on comprehension, application, and clarification of productive skills.

VOCABULARY STRATEGIES

Vocabulary strategy sections focus on form, use, and meaning to help students process complex content.

TRANSITION LEVEL

CEFR	GSE
B2+–C1	68–80

A deep dive for transition-level students, the Transition level mirrors the academic rigor of college courses.

INTENSIVE SKILL PRACTICE

Intensive skill practice tied to learning objectives informed by the Global Scale of English

AUTHENTIC CONTENT

- Readings: 200–3,500-words
- Lectures: 25 minutes

CONTENT AND FLUENCY VOCABULARY APPROACH

- No direct vocabulary instruction
- Online vocabulary practice for remediation

Key Features

A consistent and systematic format in every chapter enables students to build confidence as they master essential fundamental and critical thinking skills.

CHAPTER STRUCTURE	
CHAPTER PROFILE	This overview establishes context with visuals to provide interest and schema-building.
OUTCOMES	Sequenced, recycled, and carefully integrated, outcomes focus on developing language skills and are informed by Pearson's Global Scale of English.
GETTING STARTED	A set of discussion questions activates learner schema and motivates students to engage with the content.
READ	The thematically-related readings highlight key concepts. These are preceded by a reading skill presentation and followed by critical thinking, collaboration, and practical application tasks.
WRITE	Modes for authentic academic writing tasks with careful step-by-step writing instruction, tied to learner outcomes, prepare students to integrate content, grammar, and vocabulary as they move through the stages of the writing process.
GRAMMAR FOR WRITING	Dedicated grammar presentation and practices prepare students for authentic writing tasks.
BUILDING VOCABULARY	Thematically-related vocabulary instruction and practice that helps students further their understanding of word grammar and expand their vocabulary.
APPLY YOUR SKILLS	Extensive practical application allows students to practice the skills developed in the chapter.
DEVELOP SOFT SKILLS	Task-based strategies focus on college readiness, social and cultural awareness, and academic study.

Students are engaged from the first page, with unit openers that feature high-interest images related to the chapter themes. Chapter openers include a stimulating content-based image and an overview of the chapter's topics and skills.

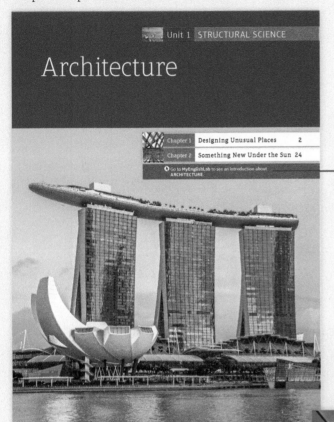

A **video introduction** at the beginning of each unit gives students an academic perspective.

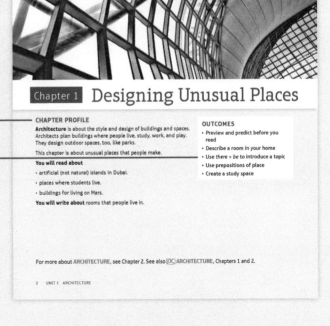

A **chapter profile** outlines the chapter content to prepare students for the reading and writing they will do in the chapter.

Outcomes aligned with the Global Scale of English are clearly stated to ensure student awareness of skills.

Engaging and high-interest readings allow students to connect with the academic content as they develop fundamental reading and critical thinking skills.

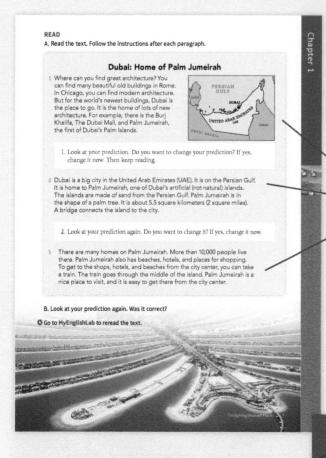

Readings are "chunked" to support the unique needs of beginning students.

Carefully scaffolded language learning **tasks** develop the language skills students need to manage more linguistically complex and conceptually challenging content as they move towards the rigor of college courses.

Tasks follow **Bloom's Taxonomy** to build, develop, and practice skills.

Tips throughout the book explain strategies to help students with reading, writing, and learning new words.

READ AGAIN

A. Read the text again. Then read the statements below. Circle T (true) or F (false).

T /F̄ 1. You can find the world's newest buildings in ~~Rome~~. *Dubai*

T / F 2. Palm Jumeirah is the only artificial island in Dubai.

T / F 3. Dubai is on the Persian Gulf.

T / F 4. Palm Jumeirah is in the shape of a palm tree.

T / F 5. Dubai is about 5.5 square kilometers.

T / F 6. Palm Jumeirah has hotels, beaches, and stores.

B. Work with a partner. Compare your answers in Part A. Correct the false statements.

C. Circle the answer.

What's the main idea of the text?

a. Palm Jumeirah is an interesting place in Dubai.

b. The beaches on Palm Jumeirah are easy to get to.

c. Many cities in the world have modern architecture.

D. Read the questions. Discuss them with a partner.

1. Is it interesting to read about Palm Jumeirah? Why or why not?

2. What places in the world do you want to visit? Why?

E. Read the questions. Discuss them with the class.

1. How do you preview an article? What do you look at?

2. Is predicting easy? Does it help you to understand a reading? Why or why not?

TIP

It is a good idea to reread a text. After you read it for the second time, you will understand it better and remember more about it.

Writing skills prepare students for the complexity and challenges of the higher levels and authentic academic writing. Writing skills include telling stories using time signals, using descriptive language, using spatial order to describe visuals, and describing a process.

WRITE

SKILL: CONNECTING IDEAS BETWEEN SENTENCES

A sentence expresses a simple idea about a topic. To say more about a topic, you can write a **paragraph**. A paragraph is a group of sentences that work together to express a bigger idea—a main idea.

> **TIP**
>
> A paragraph is not a list of sentences. It looks different. When you write a paragraph, begin each new sentence right after the sentence before it, on the same line.

Connecting the ideas in a paragraph is important. Well-connected sentences make your ideas easier to understand. In a paragraph about a series of events, use time signal words to show the order of events. Look at the example and notice the boldfaced words.

> Kai does the same things every weekday morning. He wakes up **at 7 A.M.** He brushes his teeth, **and then** he takes a shower. **After his shower**, he eats breakfast. **Then** he leaves for work. He usually takes the bus, but he takes his bike when the weather is nice. He gets to work **at 9:15, and then** he starts his workday.

The paragraph about Kai's routine is easy to understand for these reasons:

1. The subject (*Kai*, or *he*) is the same throughout the paragraph.

2. The events are connected to each other in order.

3. The time markers and the signal words, like *then* and *after*, guide the reader, showing the order of events. For example, notice that after *takes a shower,* you find *After his shower*. The writer uses *After his shower* to clearly connect the events in the two sentences.

Study the chart.

	Example	Order of Events
then	She showers. **Then** she eats breakfast	1. She showers. 2. She eats breakfast.
before + noun	**Before class**, I always have a cup of coffee.	1. I have coffee. 2. Class starts.
after + noun	**After work**, I exercise.	1. Work finishes. 2. I exercise.
finally	She reads a book in bed. **Finally,** around 11 P.M., she falls asleep.	1. She reads. 2. She falls asleep.

REMEMBER

Complete the sentences.

1. You must make your writing _____ to understand.

2. Connect ideas and events by using signal words like *then* and *next*. You can also use the words _____ and _____ + a noun to show the order of events.

Clear and concise **presentations** help students focus on the target skill.

Writing **models** feature chapter-based writing skill and grammar targets, giving students a reference for upcoming writing tasks.

Throughout each chapter, **examples**, **charts**, and **images** support understanding of concepts and vocabulary.

Remember boxes allow students to demonstrate understanding of the skill.

Students are introduced to the writing process with step-by-step writing instruction, tied to learner outcomes.

WRITE ABOUT YOUR ROUTINE

STEP 1: READ TO WRITE

A. Read the words and definitions. You will see these words in the text.

Glossary

calorie: a measure of the amount of energy in food
competition: an event where athletes or teams play against each other
gym: a place to exercise
nap: a short sleep during the daytime
wake up: stop sleeping

B. Read the text. Follow the instructions after Paragraphs 1–3.

Everyday Routines: Olympic Swimmers

1 Olympic swimmers start their day early. Most wake up at around 6:30 A.M. and eat a really big breakfast. Next, they go to the pool and swim for a few hours. After swimming, they eat a big lunch. In fact, Olympic swimmers eat more than 10,000 calories a day. Compared to most Americans, this is a lot. The average American eats about 3,500 calories a day.

An Olympic swimmer in a pool

> Step 1 exposes students to a **model** of authentic academic writing.

> A **glossary** features challenging vocabulary items essential for understanding the text.

STEP 2: PREPARE TO WRITE

A. Read the questions. Discuss them with a partner or in a small group.

1. Do you have a morning routine? That is, do you have a routine between waking up and leaving your home? Describe it.

2. Do you have routines at school or work? Describe your usual routine for one day.

3. Do you have a nighttime routine? That is, do you have a routine between coming home and going to bed? Describe it.

4. Do you have any other routines? Maybe a study routine or an exercise routine? Describe it.

B. Write notes about a routine you follow.

My Routine	
Time	Event

> Step 2 prepares students for the writing task. Extensive use of **graphic organizers** support students through the writing process.

STEP 3: WRITE

Write a paragraph of 5 or more sentences about a routine of yours. Follow these instructions:

• Do not include the times of everything that you do. Use time signal words like *then*, *before*, and *after* to connect the ideas.

> In Step 3, students integrate content, writing skills, grammar, and vocabulary as they move through **the writing process**.

STEP 4: PROOFREAD AND EDIT

A. Proofread your paragraph.

• Do you focus on one topic (your routine) in your writing?

• Do you use words that show order (for example, *before*, *then*, and *next*)?

• Do you use adverbs of frequency? Do you use *every*?

• Are there any spelling mistakes?

B. Work with your partner. Share your paragraphs. Answer the questions in the Peer Review Form. Share feedback. Then edit your sentences.

Peer Review Form	Yes	No
1. Does your partner write about his or her routine in a clear way?	☐	☐
2. Does your partner focus on one topic in his or her writing?	☐	☐
3. Does your partner use words that show order?	☐	☐
4. Are the sentences in the form of a paragraph?	☐	☐
5. Are there any spelling mistakes? If there are, circle them.	☐	☐

> Step 4 guides students through the **editing and proofreading** aspects of the writing process, including **peer review**.

Dedicated grammar presentation and practice prepare students for authentic writing tasks. Tasks focus on form, use, and meaning and move from controlled to practical application.

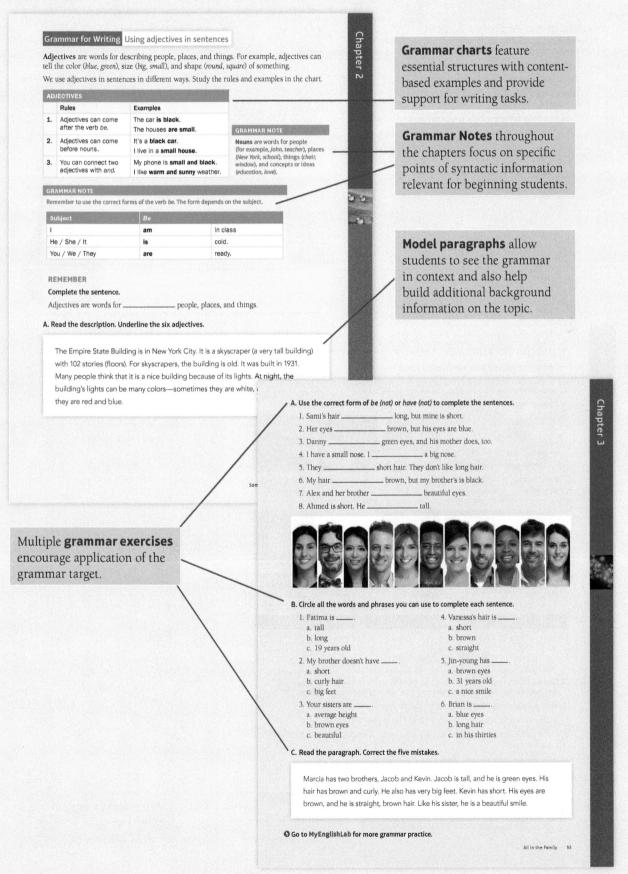

Grammar charts feature essential structures with content-based examples and provide support for writing tasks.

Grammar Notes throughout the chapters focus on specific points of syntactic information relevant for beginning students.

Model paragraphs allow students to see the grammar in context and also help build additional background information on the topic.

Multiple **grammar exercises** encourage application of the grammar target.

The following text appears within the sample pages shown:

Grammar for Writing Using adjectives in sentences

Adjectives are words for describing people, places, and things. For example, adjectives can tell the color (*blue, green*), size (*big, small*), and shape (*round, square*) of something.

We use adjectives in sentences in different ways. Study the rules and examples in the chart.

ADJECTIVES

	Rules	Examples
1.	Adjectives can come after the verb *be*.	The car **is black**. The houses **are small**.
2.	Adjectives can come before nouns.	It's a **black car**. I live in a **small house**.
3.	You can connect two adjectives with *and*.	My phone is **small and black**. I like **warm and sunny** weather.

GRAMMAR NOTE

Nouns are words for people (for example, *John, teacher*), places (*New York, school*), things (*chair, window*), and concepts or ideas (*education, love*).

GRAMMAR NOTE

Remember to use the correct forms of the verb *be*. The form depends on the subject.

Subject	Be	
I	**am**	in class
He / She / It	**is**	cold.
You / We / They	**are**	ready.

REMEMBER

Complete the sentence.

Adjectives are words for _____ people, places, and things.

A. Read the description. Underline the six adjectives.

The Empire State Building is in New York City. It is a skyscraper (a very tall building) with 102 stories (floors). For skyscrapers, the building is old. It was built in 1931. Many people think that it is a nice building because of its lights. At night, the building's lights can be many colors—sometimes they are white, a they are red and blue.

A. Use the correct form of *be (not)* or *have (not)* to complete the sentences.

1. Sami's hair _____ long, but mine is short.
2. Her eyes _____ brown, but his eyes are blue.
3. Danny _____ green eyes, and his mother does, too.
4. I have a small nose. I _____ a big nose.
5. They _____ short hair. They don't like long hair.
6. My hair _____ brown, but my brother's is black.
7. Alex and her brother _____ beautiful eyes.
8. Ahmed is short. He _____ tall.

B. Circle all the words and phrases you can use to complete each sentence.

1. Fatima is ____.
   a. tall
   b. long
   c. 19 years old

2. My brother doesn't have ____.
   a. short
   b. curly hair
   c. big feet

3. Your sisters are ____.
   a. average height
   b. brown eyes
   c. beautiful

4. Vanessa's hair is ____.
   a. short
   b. brown
   c. straight

5. Jin-young has ____.
   a. brown eyes
   b. 31 years old
   c. a nice smile

6. Brian is ____.
   a. blue eyes
   b. long hair
   c. in his thirties

C. Read the paragraph. Correct the five mistakes.

Marcia has two brothers, Jacob and Kevin. Jacob is tall, and he is green eyes. His hair has brown and curly. He also has very big feet. Kevin has short. His eyes are brown, and he is straight, brown hair. Like his sister, he is a beautiful smile.

◐ Go to MyEnglishLab for more grammar practice.

All in the Family   55

A mix of academic and high-frequency vocabulary provides the fundamental building blocks with which students can read and discern texts and construct meaningful writing.

VOCABULARY PREVIEW

A. Read the sentences. Look at the boldfaced words and phrases. Do you know what they mean? Share your ideas with a partner.

1. Modern life is easier because of science and **technology**.
2. The Finolhu Villas **are located** in the Maldives.
3. There are big windows on the front, back, and **sides** of the building.
4. People like parks and other **green spaces** in their cities.

VOCABULARY NOTE

Tech is a short form of *technology.* You will often see *tech* used as an adjective before a noun, as in *tech company. Tech* can also be a noun, as in *The phone has all the newest tech.*

Vocabulary Notes throughout the text include helpful information on the meanings and uses of words and phrases.

Explicit vocabulary instruction includes **Previews** and **Reviews** that appear before and after each reading.

VOCABULARY REVIEW

Complete the sentences with the words and phrases from the box.

beach	kilometers	sand	the middle of
connects	modern	shape	

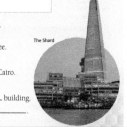

The Shard

1. There are many people at the _____. Some people are swimming in the water.
2. Palm Jumeirah has the _____ of a tree.
3. A long road _____ the two cities.
4. The Nile River goes through _____ Cairo.
5. Dubai is about 4,000 square _____.
6. The Shard in London is a very _____ building.
7. A beach can have millions of grains of _____. Each grain is very small.

BUILDING VOCABULARY

USING MORE WORDS FOR DESCRIBING FOOD

There are many words related to food. In this section, you will learn words for types of food, ways of cooking, and food textures (like *soft* and *hard*).

A. Look at the photos. Put the boldfaced words into the correct columns in the chart.

Some people love **seafood**.

Dairy foods include cheese, milk, and yogurt.

Pizza can be an **oily** food.

People eat **boiled** potatoes all around the world.

Grilled chicken tastes good.

Potato chips are **crunchy**. They make a loud sound.

I eat **fried** eggs every morning.

Macaroni and cheese is a very **creamy** food.

People all over the world eat **nuts**.

These **steamed** dumplings are called *manti*.

Textures	Types of food	Ways of cooking food
oily		

Building Vocabulary sections help students understand new words and phrases related to the themes. Engaging practice activities follow the presentation.

B. Can you think of more words for textures, types of foods, and ways of cooking? Add them to the chart. Then compare your lists with a partner or small group.

C. Read the questions. Discuss them with a partner or in a small group.

1. Do you like seafood? What kinds of seafood do you like? How about dairy?
2. Are grilled foods healthy? Do you like grilled foods? How about steamed, fried, or boiled foods?
3. Do you like crunchy foods? How about oily or creamy foods?

◯ Go to **MyEnglishLab** to complete a vocabulary practice.

CULTURE NOTE

Vegetarians do not eat meat or fish. Some people do not eat meat, fish, or any food that comes from an animal, like milk, eggs, or honey. These people are called **vegans**. The word *vegan* can be a noun or adjective. You can say, *Jaime is a vegan* (noun) or *This soup is vegan* (adjective).

Culture Notes expand understanding of a broad range of cultural topics.

80   UNIT 2   GENETICS

Each chapter concludes with an Apply Your skills section that includes practical application of the reading, writing, vocabulary, and grammar skills students have been studying. This section can also function as an assessment.

APPLY YOUR SKILLS

In this chapter, you read about instructions and processes, and you learned about the buyer decision process and the process for returning an item ordered from an e-commerce site. You also wrote instructions on how to create an account for an e-commerce site or a profile for another type of site. In Apply Your Skills, you will learn about cybersecurity: protecting your information on your mobile devices and online.

The **introduction** to APPLY YOUR SKILLS starts with a recap of the chapter so far and provides a preview of what is to come.

PREDICT

Privacy (keeping your information safe from others) is important. How do you keep the information on your phone safe? How do you protect your privacy? Check (✓) all your answers.

☐ I use passwords for my phone.

☐ I must enter a password before I can use my apps.

☐ I don't use social media.

☐ I don't share much information on social media sites.

☐ I sign out of my email and other accounts when I finish using them.

☐ I don't use WiFi outside of my home and school.

Vocabulary Preview and **Predict** activities precede the reading.

READ

A. Read the text. Answer the question after each paragraph.

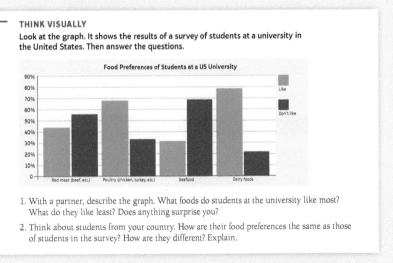

TechNow — YOUR VIEW   WORLD VIEW   CONNECT   MORE

I Got Hacked—Protect Yourself!

1   Somebody hacked my online account for the WebShopping site a few months ago—what a terrible experience! They stole my credit card number and my social security number. With that information, they signed up for at least three new credit cards in my name. But luckily, WebShopping learned about the problem and emailed me about it. After many hours on the phone, I canceled all my credit cards and fixed the problem. I don't want to get hacked again, and I don't want you to get hacked. So here are a few tips for protecting your privacy.

1. Which statement is true?

   a. The writer works for a company called WebShopping.

   b. The writer wants to help people to protect their personal information.

(Continued)

Longer reading passages allow students to apply skills practiced in the chapter.

Think Visually provides an opportunity for students to analyze charts, graphs, photos, and other visuals.

THINK VISUALLY

Look at the graph. It shows the results of a survey of students at a university in the United States. Then answer the questions.

Food Preferences of Students at a US University

Like / Don't like

Red meat (beef, etc.) · Poultry (chicken, turkey, etc.) · Seafood · Dairy foods

1. With a partner, describe the graph. What foods do students at the university like most? What do they like least? Does anything surprise you?

2. Think about students from your country. How are their food preferences the same as those of students in the survey? How are they different? Explain.

Strategies for academic success, life skills, and career readiness skills—using graphic organizers, communicating with instructors, and giving peer feedback—appear in each chapter. These soft skills help increase students' confidence and ability to cope with challenges of academic study and college culture.

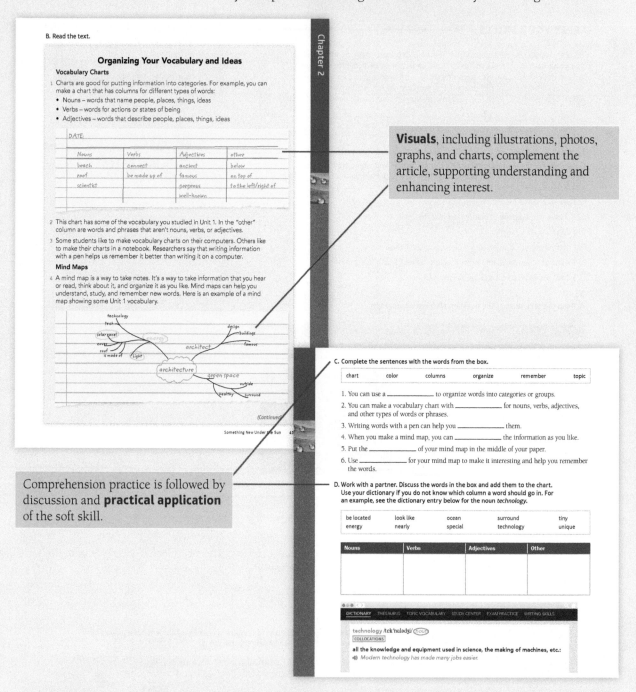

Visuals, including illustrations, photos, graphs, and charts, complement the article, supporting understanding and enhancing interest.

Comprehension practice is followed by discussion and **practical application** of the soft skill.

WHAT DID YOU LEARN?

At the end of each chapter, students complete a **skill self-assessment** checklist.

SKILLS

☐ I can preview and predict before reading.

☐ I can describe a room in my home.

☐ I can use *there + be* to introduce a topic.

☐ I can use prepositions of place.

☐ I can create a study space.

A BLENDED APPROACH

University Success integrates a tailored online lab populated with engaging multimedia content including videos, slide presentations, and audio, which can be used for presenting new content and skills, as well as practice and extension activities for students to complete in class or as homework. All MyEnglishLab activities are referenced throughout the Student Books.

MyEnglishLab includes an easy-to-use online management system that offers a flexible gradebook and tools for monitoring student success.

TEACHER RESOURCES

Downloadable step-by-step teaching notes for each chapter offer suggestions and a "library" of teaching tips for teaching skills and content

Essential tools such as audio scripts, answer keys, and course planners help in lesson planning

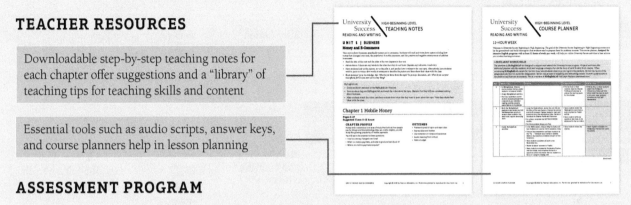

ASSESSMENT PROGRAM

University Success has several different types of assessments that provide opportunities for teachers to gauge learning. These assessments can be used as pre-course diagnostics, chapter achievement tests, mid-course assessments, and final summative assessments. The flexible nature of these assessments allows teachers to choose which assessments will be most appropriate at various stages of the program. Two different versions of these assessments are available in MyEnglishLab, in both Word and PDF formats. There are formative assessments embedded in the Student Book.

HOW WOULD YOU LIKE TO ASSESS YOUR STUDENTS?

Assessment	Where to Find	How to Use
Skill Self-Assessments	MyEnglishLab	• At the beginning and end of every chapter for students to identify skill areas for improvement • To provide data that can inform lesson planning
Achievement Tests	MyEnglishLab	• As a summative assessment at the end of each chapter
Apply Your Skills	Student Book	• As a diagnostic assessment to inform students' strengths and weaknesses before they complete a chapter • As a formative assessment, in which students complete this section or parts of this section after they complete the chapter
Mid-Term Exam	MyEnglishLab	• As a summative assessment at the end of Units 1 and 2
Final Exam	MyEnglsihLab	• As a summative assessment at the end of Units 3 and 4
Writing / Speaking Skill Assessment	Student Book	• Writing and Speaking Tasks: As formative assessments to evaluate practical application of skills presented
Vocabulary Quiz	Student Book	• *Vocabulary Previews / Reviews:* As a diagnostic to inform teaching and lesson planning • As formative assessments to assess student understanding of vocabulary
Grammar Quiz	Student Book	• *Grammar tasks:* As a diagnostic to identify student understanding of grammar points • As formative assessments to assess student understanding of grammar points
Skill, Vocabulary, Grammar Assessments	MyEnglishLab	• Any activity in MyEnglishLab to be used as formative assessments to assess student understanding of chapter-related content

Scope and Sequence

GRAMMAR SKILLS	BUILDING VOCABULARY	SOFT SKILLS	MYENGLISHLAB
			Video: An Introduction about Architecture
Use *there is / there are*	Use prepositions of place	Create a study space TASK Describe your study space	Skill self-assessments Online practice: • reading • grammar • vocabulary
Use adjectives in sentences	Understand synonyms and antonyms	Use graphic organizers to study vocabulary TASK Make a mind map	Skill self-assessments Online practice: • reading • grammar • vocabulary Challenge reading: **The Learning Hub in Singapore**
			Video: An Introduction about Genetics
Use *have* and *be* in descriptions	Describe physical appearance	Work in groups TASK Describe your group work skills	Skill self-assessments Online practice: • reading • grammar • vocabulary
Use count and noncount nouns	Use more words for describing food	Stay healthy TASK Write tips for college students on staying healthy	Skill self-assessments Online practice: • reading • grammar • vocabulary Challenge reading: **Nutrigenomics and Health**
			Video: An Introduction about Business and Technology
Use *can* for ability and possibility	Use vocabulary for smartphone users	Communicate with instructors TASK Write an email to your instructor	Skill self-assessments Online practice: • reading • grammar • vocabulary
Use possessive adjectives	Use tech-related phrasal verbs	Give peer feedback TASK Prepare to give peer feedback outside of class	Skill self-assessments Online practice: • reading • grammar • vocabulary Challenge reading: **Then and Now: Music and Business**
			Video: An Introduction about Psychology
Use adverbs of frequency and *every*	Use vocabulary for daily activities	Make healthy choices TASK Write about exercise in your daily life	Skill self-assessments Online practice: • reading • grammar • vocabulary
Use the simple past	Understand suffixes	Use flashcards to learn new vocabulary TASK Make a flashcard	Skill self-assessments Online practice: • reading • grammar • vocabulary Challenge reading: **Why Doesn't Everyone Remember Their Dreams?**

Acknowledgments

I'd like to thank all the people at Pearson who made this book happen. Special thanks to Amy McCormick for inviting me to take part, and to Christen Savage for always having a good idea when I didn't. And a big thank you to Debbie Sistino for just about everything else. Of course, thanks to all the brilliant and hardworking students, teachers, and administrators at the American Language Program, Columbia University—without their support and inspiration, I'd have nothing to put in this book! And one last thank you to Megan and Rodrigo, for everything they do.

—Tim McLaughlin

Reviewers

We would like to thank the following reviewers for their many helpful comments and suggestions:

Jamila Barton, North Seattle Community College, Seattle, WA; **Joan Chamberlin**, Iowa State University, Ames IA; **Lyam Christopher**, Palm Beach State College, Boynton Beach, FL; **Robin Corcos**, University of California, Santa Barbara, Goleta, CA; **Tanya Davis**, University of California, San Diego, CA; **Brendan DeCoster**, University of Oregon, Eugene, OR; **Thomas Dougherty**, University of St. Mary of the Lake, Mundelein, IL; **Bina Dugan**, Bergen County Community College, Hackensack, NJ; **Bonnie Duhart**, Lone Star College, University Park, TX; **Priscilla Faucette**, University of Hawaii at Manoa, Honolulu, HI; **Lisa Fischer**, St. Louis University, St. Louis, MO; **Kathleen Flynn**, Glendale Community College, Glendale, CA; **Mary Gawienowski**, William Rainey Harper College, Palatine, IL; **Sally Gearhart**, Santa Rosa Junior College, Santa Rosa, CA; **Carl Guerriere**, Capital Community College, Hartford, CT; **Vera Guillen**, Eastfield College, Mesquite, TX; **Angela Hakim**, St. Louis University, St. Louis, MO; **Pamela Hartmann**, Evans Community Adult School, Los Angeles Unified School District, Los Angeles, CA; **Shelly Hedstrom**, Palm Beach State University, Lake Worth, FL; **Sherie Henderson**, University of Oregon, Eugene, OR; **Lisse Hildebrandt**, English Language Program, Virginia Commonwealth University, Richmond, VA; **Barbara Inerfeld**, Rutgers University, Piscataway, NJ; **Bessie Karras-Lazaris**, California State University, Northridge, CA; **Zaimah Khan**, Northern Virginia Community College, Loudon Campus, Sterling, VA; **Tricia Kinman**, St. Louis University, St. Louis, MO; **Kathleen Klaiber**, Genesee Community College, Batavia, NY; **Kevin Lamkins**, Capital Community College, Hartford, CT; **Noga Laor**, Long Island University, Brooklyn, NY; **Mayetta Lee**, Palm Beach State College, Lake Worth, FL; **Kirsten Lillegard**, English Language Institute, Divine Word College, Epworth, IA; **Craig Machado**, Norwalk Community College, Norwalk, CT; **Cheryl Madrid**, Spring International Language Center, Denver, CO; **Ann Meechai**, St. Louis University, St. Louis, MO; **Melissa Mendelson**, Department of Linguistics, University of Utah, Salt Lake City, UT; **Tamara Milbourn**, University of Colorado, Boulder, CO; **Debbie Ockey**, Fresno City College, Fresno, CA; **Diana Pascoe-Chavez**, St. Louis University, St. Louis, MO; **Raymond Purdy**, ELS Language Centers, Princeton, NJ; **Kathleen Reynolds**, William Rainey Harper College, Palatine, IL; **Linda Roth**, Vanderbilt University ELC, Greensboro, NC; **Minati Roychoudhuri**, Capital Community College, Hartford, CT; **Bruce Rubin**, California State University, Fullerton, CA; **Margo Sampson**, Syracuse University, Syracuse, NY; **Elena Sapp**, Oregon State University, Corvallis, OR; **Sarah Saxer**, Howard Community College, Ellicott City, MD; **Anne-Marie Schlender**, Austin Community College, Austin, TX; **Susan Shields**, Santa Barbara Community College, Santa Barbara, CA; **Barbara Smith-Palinkas**, Hillsborough Community College, Dale Mabry Campus, Tampa, FL; **Sara Stapleton**, North Seattle Community College, Seattle, WA; **Lisa Stelle**, Northern Virginia Community College Loudon, Sterling, VA; **Jamie Tanzman**, Northern Kentucky University, Highland Heights, KY; **Ariana Van Beurden**, Oregon State University, Corvallis, OR; **Jeffrey Welliver**, Soka University of America, Aliso Viejo, CA; **Mark Wolfersberger**, Brigham Young University, Hawaii, Laie, HI; **May Youn**, California State University, Fullerton, CA

Architecture

 Go to **MyEnglishLab** to see an introduction about **ARCHITECTURE**.

Designing Unusual Places

CHAPTER PROFILE

Architecture is about the style and design of buildings and spaces. Architects plan buildings where people live, study, work, and play. They design outdoor spaces, too, like parks.

This chapter is about unusual places that people make.

You will read about

• artificial (not natural) islands in Dubai.

• places where students live.

• buildings for living on Mars.

You will write about rooms that people live in.

OUTCOMES

• Preview and predict before you read

• Describe a room in your home

• Use *there + be* to introduce a topic

• Use prepositions of place

• Create a study space

For more about **ARCHITECTURE**, see Chapter 2. See also [OC] **ARCHITECTURE**, Chapters 1 and 2.

GETTING STARTED

Work with a partner. Look at the photos below and answer the questions.

1. Do you know of these places? Where are they?

2. Do you want to visit these places? Why or why not?

○ Go to **MyEnglishLab** to complete a self-assessment.

READ

SKILL: PREVIEWING AND PREDICTING

How do you get ready to read a text? Before you read, it's a good idea to **preview** the text. When you preview, look at the title and pictures. What do they tell you about the text?

After you preview, make **predictions** about the text. Guess: What will the text be about? Write the predictions down, and come back to them after reading.

For example, look at the title and photo below. Which is a good prediction about the text?

a. The reading is about parks in Chicago.

b. The reading is about buildings in Chicago.

Chicago: America's Architectural City

Chicago is one of the biggest cities in the United States. It is known across the world for …

Did you choose *b*? If yes, then your prediction is probably good. The word *Architectural* tells us the text will probably be about buildings.

Remember your predictions when you read. You can change your predictions as you read.

Previewing and predicting help you think about a text before you read it. They help you to understand it better.

REMEMBER

Complete the sentences.

_____ a text before you read. Then make _____ about the text.

VOCABULARY PREVIEW

A. Read the sentences. Look at the boldfaced words and phrases. Do you know what they mean? Share your ideas with a partner.

1. A bridge **connects** the islands to the city.

2. It is 1,250 **kilometers** from New York to Chicago.

3. The Burj Khalifa is a **modern** building.

4. There's a lot of **sand** at the **beach**.

5. The letter H is in **the middle of** the keyboard.

6. The plate has the **shape** of a heart.

Sand on a beach

B. Write the boldfaced words and phrases from Part A next to their definitions.

_____ 1. new, of the present time

_____ 2. very small pieces of rock that you find at beaches or in deserts

_____ 3. the center of, not near the sides of

_____ 4. a place with sand near an ocean or lake

_____ 5. the form of something (such as round or square)

_____ 6. a way to measure how far it is between two places

_____ 7. joins two or more things or places together

A plate in the shape of a heart

🔊 Go to **MyEnglishLab** to complete a vocabulary practice.

PREDICT

Look at the title of the text, the map below it, and the photo on page 5. Complete the prediction about the text. Circle *a* or *b*.

The text will be about _____ .

a. buildings around the world

b. architecture in Dubai

A. Read the text. Follow the instructions after each paragraph.

Dubai: Home of Palm Jumeirah

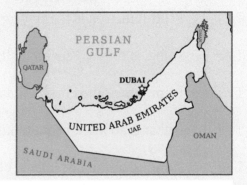

1 Where can you find great architecture? You can find many beautiful old buildings in Rome. In Chicago, you can find modern architecture. But for the world's newest buildings, Dubai is the place to go. It is the home of lots of new architecture. For example, there is the Burj Khalifa, The Dubai Mall, and Palm Jumeirah, the first of Dubai's Palm Islands.

1. Look at your prediction. Do you want to change your prediction? If yes, change it now. Then keep reading.

2 Dubai is a big city in the United Arab Emirates (UAE). It is on the Persian Gulf. It is home to Palm Jumeirah, one of Dubai's artificial (not natural) islands. The islands are made of sand from the Persian Gulf. Palm Jumeirah is in the shape of a palm tree. It is about 5.5 square kilometers (2 square miles). A bridge connects the island to the city.

2. Look at your prediction again. Do you want to change it? If yes, change it now.

3 There are many homes on Palm Jumeirah. More than 10,000 people live there. Palm Jumeirah also has beaches, hotels, and places for shopping. To get to the shops, hotels, and beaches from the city center, you can take a train. The train goes through the middle of the island. Palm Jumeirah is a nice place to visit, and it is easy to get there from the city center.

B. Look at your prediction again. Was it correct?

⬆ Go to **MyEnglishLab** to reread the text.

READ AGAIN

A. Read the text again. Then read the statements below. Circle *T* (true) or *F* (false).

T / ~~F~~   1. You can find the world's newest buildings in ~~Rome~~. *Dubai*

T / F   2. Palm Jumeirah is the only artificial island in Dubai.

T / F   3. Dubai is on the Persian Gulf.

T / F   4. Palm Jumeirah is in the shape of a palm tree.

T / F   5. Dubai is about 5.5 square kilometers.

T / F   6. Palm Jumeirah has hotels, beaches, and stores.

B. Work with a partner. Compare your answers in Part A. Correct the false statements.

C. Circle the answer.

What's the main idea of the text?

a. Palm Jumeirah is an interesting place in Dubai.

b. The beaches on Palm Jumeirah are easy to get to.

c. Many cities in the world have modern architecture.

D. Read the questions. Discuss them with a partner.

1. Is it interesting to read about Palm Jumeirah? Why or why not?

2. What places in the world do you want to visit? Why?

E. Read the questions. Discuss them with the class.

1. How do you preview an article? What do you look at?

2. Is predicting easy? Does it help you to understand a reading? Why or why not?

TIP

It is a good idea to reread a text. After you read it for the second time, you will understand it better and remember more about it.

VOCABULARY REVIEW

Complete the sentences with the words and phrases from the box.

beach	kilometers	sand	the middle of
connects	modern	shape	

The Shard

1. There are many people at the _____ .
   Some people are swimming in the water.
2. Palm Jumeirah has the _____ of a tree.
3. A long road _____ the two cities.
4. The Nile River goes through _____ Cairo.
5. Dubai is about 4,000 square _____ .
6. The Shard in London is a very _____ building.
7. A beach can have millions of grains of _____ .
   Each grain is very small.

⚓ Go to **MyEnglishLab** to read another text.

WRITE

SKILL: DESCRIBING A ROOM

Describing a room is easy. First, think about the things in the room. What do you see first? Is it a window? A bed? Usually it will be the biggest thing in the room. Describe its location (where it is) first. Is it in the middle of the room? Is it on the left or on the right? Then describe something that is close to it.

Look at the photo of the room and the sentences that describe it.

This is a college dorm room.

There are two beds in it.

One bed is in front of the window.

There is a small table next to each bed.

There are lamps on each table.

There is a rug on the floor.

REMEMBER

Complete the sentence.

When you write about a room, describe the _____ of the biggest thing in the room first.

Grammar for Writing Using *there is / there are*

Use **there is** and **there are** to introduce a topic. Use them when you write about a person or thing for the first time. *There is* introduces one person or thing, and *there are* introduces more than one person or thing.

We often use *there is* and *there are* to describe a location.

THERE IS / THERE ARE

Affirmative Statements

There + be	Noun	Location
There is	a family	in the kitchen.
There's	food	on the table.
There are	three people	in the room.
	eggs	in the white bowl.

Negative Statements

There + be + not	Noun	Location
There isn't	a TV	in the photo.
	any bread	on the table.
There aren't	books	on the table.
	any windows	in the photo.

GRAMMAR NOTE

After *there are*, you can use *no* to mean "zero (0)."

There are no books on the table.	=	There aren't any books on the table.
There are no flowers in the room.	=	There aren't any flowers in the room.

THERE IS / THERE ARE VS. IT IS / THEY ARE

Rules	Examples
Use *there + be* to introduce a topic. After that, use *it* or *they + be*.	**There are** two windows in my bedroom. **They are (They're)** very big.
	There is a table between the windows. **It is (It's)** small.

REMEMBER

Complete the sentences.

Use _____ for one person or thing. Use _____ for two or more people or things.

A. Circle the correct words to complete the sentences.

1. **There is / It is** a desk in my room. **There is / It is** next to a window.
2. There **is / are** a phone on the desk.
3. There **isn't / aren't** any tables in the room.
4. **There are / They are** two windows in my room. **There are / They are** big.
5. There **is / are** four chairs in the room.
6. There **is / are** a bed between the windows. **There's / It's** new.
7. There **isn't / aren't** a shirt on the bed.
8. **There are / They are** shoes under the bed.

B. Complete the sentences about the classroom in the photo.
   Use *there is (not)* or *there are (not)*.

1. _____ tables in the room.
2. _____ many chairs in the room.
3. _____ a teacher in the room.
4. _____ any students in the room.
5. _____ two windows on the right.
6. _____ a desk for the teacher near the windows.
7. _____ two screens at the front of the room.
8. _____ any books, papers, or computers on the tables.

C. Read the paragraph. Correct the eight mistakes.

I love my room. There is two big windows on the right side of the room. It's a sofa between the two windows. There are a bed on the left side of the room. I also have a desk. It's on the left, next to the bed. There are a computer on the desk, and it's a printer behind the computer. They are chargers on the desk, too. They're to the right of the computer. They aren't any books on the desk. They're on my bookcase. There is next to the desk.

○ Go to **MyEnglishLab** for more grammar practice.

WRITE A DESCRIPTION OF A ROOM

STEP 1: READ TO WRITE

A. Read the words and definitions. You will see these words in the text.

> Glossary
>
> apartment: a part of a building where people live
>
> campus: the land and buildings of a college or university
>
> dorm: a large building where students live on campus, short for *dormitory*
>
> space: an area that is empty and can be used
>
> university: a place where students study a subject at a high level

CULTURE NOTE

About 70 percent of the students who finish high school in the United States then enter a college or university. People usually call them all *college students,* and dorms on both college and university campuses are usually called *college dorms.* People also use *school* to refer to both colleges and universities, as in "Where do you go to school?" "I go to Boston University."

B. Read the description. Complete the sentence after each paragraph.

Dorm Rooms

1 College students live in different places. Some students live at home, and others live in apartments near their college or university. But many live on campus. They live in dorms. Dorm rooms are usually very small, so students try to use the space well.

1. Paragraph 1 is about _____ .

2 The dorm room in the picture has many things in it. From the front of the room, you can see a big window. There is a sofa in front of the window. To the right, there is a bed, and there is a desk under it. The other bed is against the left wall. Above this bed, there are hooks on the wall, and there are clothes on the hooks. The high bed and the hooks help save space.

2. The description in Paragraph 2 tells us about a window, a sofa, _____ , _____ , _____ , and _____ .

3 There are a few things on the desk. The computer is on the left, and on the right, there is a small bookcase with books on the shelves. Under the desk, there is a storage cart. It has four drawers to put things in. A storage cart under the desk helps to save space in the room.

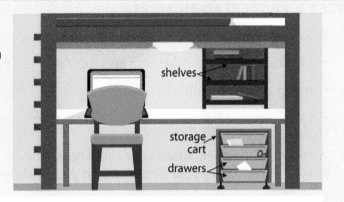

3. There is a _____ on the desk, and there are _____ on the shelves.

◑ Go to **MyEnglishLab** to reread the text.

STEP 2: PREPARE TO WRITE

Look at the picture. Read the questions. Then fill out the chart.

1. What is the first thing that you see?

2. What other objects are in the room?

	Object	Location
The first thing you see:	a bed	next to the desk
Other objects:		

STEP 3: WRITE

Write sentences about five things in the room. Use *there is* or *there are*. Tell where the things are.

1. There *is a bed in the room. It's next to the desk.* _____
2. _____
3. _____
4. _____
5. _____

STEP 4: PROOFREAD AND EDIT

A. Proofread your sentences.

- Do you use *there is / there are* and *it is / they are* correctly?

- Are there any spelling mistakes?

- Does every sentence begin with a capital letter and end with a period?

B. Work with a partner. Share your sentences. Answer the questions in the Peer Review Form. Share your answers with your partner. Ask your partner about your sentences. Then edit them.

Peer Review Form	Yes	No
1. Does your partner write about five things in the room?	☐	☐
2. Are the location descriptions correct?	☐	☐
3. Does your partner use *there is / there are* and *it is / they are* correctly?	☐	☐
4. Are there any spelling mistakes? If there are, circle them.	☐	☐

> **TIP**
>
> After you write something, try showing it to a reader. A reader's questions and comments can help you make the piece of writing better. Ask a friend or classmate to be your reader, or visit your school's writing support center.

C. Read the questions. Discuss them with a partner.

1. When you describe a room, what do you describe first?

2. Is it easy to write about the location of things? Explain.

BUILDING VOCABULARY

USING PREPOSITIONS OF PLACE

Prepositions are useful when describing places. They help you to say where things are. Some prepositions are only one word (like *on* and *in*), and some are more than one word (like *next to*). Some other prepositions used to describe location are *under, in front of*, and *in back of*.

Look at the pictures below to see the meanings of more prepositions.

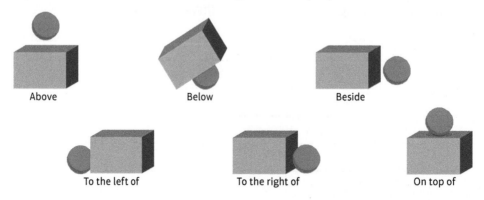

Above   Below   Beside

To the left of   To the right of   On top of

A. Look at the picture of the living room. Read the statements. Circle *T* (true) or *F* (false). Correct the false statements.

T / F   1. There is a sofa to the right of the window.

T / F   2. There is a clock below the sofa.

T / F   3. There is a small chest of drawers to the left of the sofa.

T / F   4. There are flowers beside the chest of drawers.

T / F   5. There are pictures on the wall above the chest of drawers.

T / F   6. The lights are on top of the sofa.

B. Look again at the picture of the living room. Complete the sentences with the prepositions from the box.

above	beside	on top of	to the left of	to the right of

1. There is a window _____ the sofa

2. There are lights _____ the sofa.

3. There is a clock _____ the window.

4. There is a small chest of drawers _____ the sofa.

5. There are flowers _____ the chest of drawers.

C. Write five sentences about the bedroom in this photo. Use prepositions from the pictures on page 12.

1. _____

2. _____

3. _____

4. _____

5. _____

◊ Go to **MyEnglishLab** to complete a vocabulary practice.

APPLY YOUR SKILLS

In this chapter, you read about an unusual place in Dubai, and you read about dorm rooms. You wrote sentences about things in rooms and their locations. In Apply Your Skills, you will read about an unusual place to live in Hawaii. You will also write sentences about a room in your home and the things in that room.

VOCABULARY PREVIEW

A. Read the sentences. Look at the boldfaced words. Do you know what they mean? Share your ideas with a partner.

1. People need **electricity** for their computers.

2. **Deserts** are full of sand and rocks. There isn't much water there.

3. The **planets** go around the sun. Our planet is called Earth.

4. **Scientists** study many different things, like animals and people. They work at universities and big companies.

5. Cara is very **healthy**. She eats good food and gets a lot of exercise.

6. Ray got a **perfect** score on the test—100 percent!

7. There are many trees **outside**. They're very big.

8. Balls are **round**.

B. Write the boldfaced words from Part A next to their definitions.

_____ 1. people who study or work in science (in biology, chemistry, or physics, for example)

_____ 2. hot, dry places with few plants and lots of sand

_____ 3. very good, not having any mistakes or problems

_____ 4. not sick, in good condition

_____ 5. energy that makes machines (like computers and TVs) work

_____ 6. not inside a building

_____ 7. in the shape or a circle or ball

_____ 8. large objects in space that travel around a star (like Earth around the sun)

🔊 Go to **MyEnglishLab** to complete a vocabulary practice.

PREDICT

Look at the title of the text and the pictures on pages 16 and 17. Complete the prediction about the text. Circle *a* or *b*.

The text will be about _____ .

a. the Big Island of Hawaii

b. learning to live on Mars

READ

A. Read the text. Follow the instructions after each paragraph.

HI-SEAS: Mars Living on Earth

1 When you hear the word *Hawaii*, you probably think about beautiful beaches and good weather. For some people, Hawaii is the perfect place to live. But what about the word *Mars*? You probably think about deserts and cold air. No one lives on Mars. But on the Big Island of Hawaii, there is a place that looks like Mars. In that place, there is a big round building. The people inside are learning how we could live on Mars.

THE HAWAIIAN ISLANDS
PACIFIC OCEAN
HAWAII
HI-SEAS

HI-SEAS is in Hawaii

Mars

1. Look at your prediction again. Do you want to change your prediction? If yes, change it now. Then keep reading.

2 The building is called the Hawaii Space Exploration Analog and Simulation, or HI-SEAS. (You say it like "hi sees.") It is not very big. There are only two floors. When you walk in on the first floor, there is a kitchen at the back, in the middle of the space. To the right of the kitchen, there is a table for eating. In front of the table, there are desks. To the left of the kitchen, there is a laboratory (a special room where scientists do tests). There's a bathroom in front of the laboratory.

2. Look at your prediction again. Do you want to change your prediction? If yes, change it now. Then keep reading.

HI-SEAS scientist wearing a spacesuit

3 On the second floor, there are six bedrooms and another bathroom. The bedrooms are very small, and there aren't any windows. Each bedroom has a bed, a small table, and a storage cart with drawers. It is a very small space for a person to live in.

> 3. Look at your prediction again. Do you want to change your prediction? If yes, change it now. Then keep reading.

4 The people at HI-SEAS are scientists. They study living on Mars. They wear spacesuits when they go outside. They eat and cook food like they are living on Mars. They have solar panels to get electricity. They want to know: Can people be healthy and happy living on Mars?

Solar panels

B. Look at your prediction again. Was it correct?

Go to **MyEnglishLab** to reread the text.

READ AGAIN

A. Read the text again. Then complete the sentences.

1. HI-SEAS is in _____ .

2. The HI-SEAS building is _____ .

3. There are _____ floors in the HI-SEAS building.

4. The first floor has a kitchen, desks, a table for eating, a laboratory, and a _____ .

5. The bedrooms aren't big. They're _____ .

6. HI-SEAS scientists live like they are on _____ .

B. Read the questions. Discuss them with a partner.

1. What do you look at when you preview a reading passage? Why?

2. When you read in your first language, do you make predictions before you read:
   - an article in a newspaper or magazine?
   - a text online?

3. Does making predictions help you decide what to read? Does it help you understand the text?

VOCABULARY REVIEW

Complete the sentences with the words from the box.

deserts	electricity	healthy	outside	perfect	planets	scientists

1. Not many people live in _____ .

2. Mark is not very _____ . He doesn't exercise, and he eats a lot of sugar and chocolate.

3. You need _____ to use your computer.

4. Mars is one of the _____ next to Earth.

5. _____ work in laboratories.

6. The weather is really good. Let's take a walk _____ .

7. This is the _____ apartment for me. It is big and has everything I need.

THINK VISUALLY

A. Read a paragraph from the text about HI-SEAS again.

The building is called the Hawaii Space Exploration Analog and Simulation, or HI-SEAS. (You say it like "hi sees.") It is not very big. There are only two floors. When you walk in on the first floor, there is a kitchen at the back, in the middle of the space. To the right of the kitchen, there is a table for eating. In front of the table, there are desks. To the left of the kitchen, there is a laboratory (a special room where scientists do tests). There's a bathroom in front of the laboratory.

B. Work with a partner. Look at the HI-SEAS floor plan. Add the things described in the paragraph in Part A. Draw them in the correct locations.

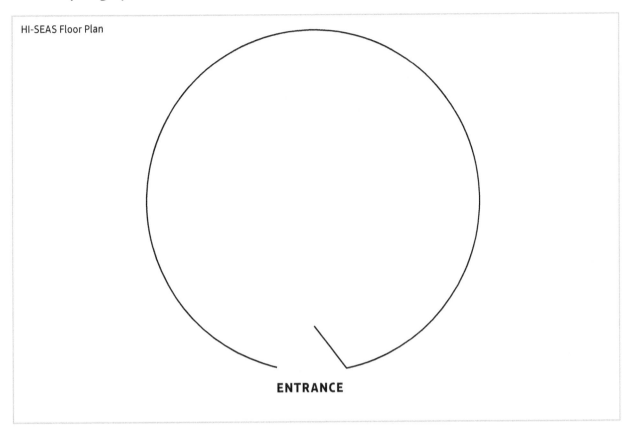

HI-SEAS Floor Plan

ENTRANCE

GRAMMAR

USING *THERE IS / THERE ARE*

Look at the picture. Complete the sentences with *there is (not) / there are (not)* or *it is (not) / they are (not).*

1. _____ a bed in the room.

2. _____ any chairs in the room.

3. _____ a blue table. _____ in front of the bed.

4. _____ two lights. _____ above the bed and the small bedside table.

5. _____ a TV in the room.

ASSIGNMENT

Write about a room in your home.

PREPARE TO WRITE

A. Think about a room in your home. What's in it? Are there chairs? Is there a desk or a bed? Draw the floor plan in the space below.

B. Work with a partner. Describe your room. Ask questions about the things in your partner's floor plan.

WRITE

Look at your floor plan of the room in your home. Write five or more sentences about your room and the things in it.

_____

_____

_____

_____

_____

_____

_____

_____

PROOFREAD AND EDIT

A. Proofread your sentences.

- Do you use *there is / there are* and *it is / they are* correctly?

- Do you use prepositions correctly?

- Are there any spelling mistakes?

B. Work with a partner. Share your sentences. Answer the questions in the Peer Review Form. Share your answers with your partner. Ask your partner about your sentences. Then edit them.

Peer Review Form	Yes	No
1. Does your partner write about the things in the room?	☐	☐
2. Are the location descriptions correct?	☐	☐
3. Does your partner use *there is / there are* and *it is / they are* correctly?	☐	☐
4. Are there any spelling mistakes? If there are, circle them.	☐	☐

⬆ Go to **MyEnglishLab** to complete grammar and vocabulary practices.

DEVELOP SOFT SKILLS

CREATING A STUDY SPACE

You can study anywhere: on the bus, in the library, or with classmates at a coffee shop. But it's important to have a good study space in your room, too. A good study space can help you learn faster and remember better. How do you make a space that is good for studying?

A. Read the words and definitions. You will see these words in the text.

Glossary

bulletin board: a board on the wall you can put notes on

comfortable chair: a chair that is easy to sit in

messy: not neat or clean

organize: put in order

suggestion: an idea someone gives you for something you can do

take a break: stop working or studying to relax for a short time

B. Read the text.

The Perfect Study Space

This desk has shelves, a drawer, and a tray for a computer keyboard.

1 It's important to have a quiet place where you can study. It's easy to create a good study space even if you are in a small dorm room or a small bedroom at home. Here are some suggestions for creating a good space to study.

- Make sure your study space is only for studying. Don't use it for anything else—for example, eating, watching TV, or playing video games.

- Be sure there is a good light. If possible, choose a space that has a window.

- Use a desk that has room for your laptop, phone, books and papers. A desk with shelves for books and drawers to put things in is best. But if you don't have a desk, a table will work, too.

- Organize everything you need at your desk. Organize the pens and pencils you like to use, your computer or tablet, paper, a dictionary, and your textbooks. A bulletin board above your desk is also a good idea.

- Pick a comfortable chair. But don't choose a chair that's easy to sleep in!

2 Other important things to remember are:

- Take breaks every 30–60 minutes. Get up out of your chair. Walk around. Maybe you can go outside for a few minutes of fresh air and exercise.

- Eat healthy snacks during your break. This will help you study better.

- Keep your study space clean. It's difficult to study at a messy desk.

- Turn off social media. Check your messages after you study!

C. Read the sentences. Circle *T* (true) or *F* (false).

T / F   1. It is important to have a big study space.

T / F   2. Use your study space to study, eat, and drink.

T / F   3. A comfortable chair will help you study better.

T / F   4. Stay at your desk when you take a break from studying.

T / F   5. Keep your study space clean.

T / F   6. Check your messages every five minutes.

D. Check (✓) the things that you like for your study space. Write two more things you like. Share your ideas with a partner.

☐ a big room   ☐ a big room

☐ a quiet space   ☐ a TV

☐ a big a big desk or table ☐ _____

☐ a comfortable chair   ☐ _____

E. Describe your study space. Write sentences about five things in your study space. Remember to proofread and edit your sentences. Share your sentences with a partner.

1. _____

2. _____

3. _____

4. _____

5. _____

WHAT DID YOU LEARN?
Check (✓) the skills and vocabulary you learned. Circle the things you need to practice.

SKILLS

☐ I can preview and predict before reading.

☐ I can describe a room in my home.

☐ I can use *there + be* to introduce a topic.

☐ I can use prepositions of place.

☐ I can create a study space.

VOCABULARY

☐ above	☐ healthy	☐ round
☐ beach	☐ kilometer	☐ sand
☐ below	☐ modern	☐ scientist
☐ beside	☐ on top of	☐ shape
☐ connect	☐ outside	☐ the middle of
☐ desert	☐ perfect	☐ to the left of
☐ electricity	☐ planet	☐ to the right of

🔊 Go to **MyEnglishLab** to complete a self-assessment.

Chapter 2 | Something New Under the Sun

CHAPTER PROFILE

When architects design buildings, they need to think about many things. Who will use the building? How will they use the building and the space around it? Where will energy for the building come from?

This chapter is about buildings and objects inside them. It is also about getting energy from the sun.

You will read about

• an unusual hotel on an island.

• solar panels.

• a famous office building in Silicon Valley.

You will write descriptions of buildings and objects.

OUTCOMES

• Scan a reading for specific information

• Describe objects

• Use adjectives in sentences

• Understand synonyms and antonyms

• Use graphic organizers to study vocabulary

For more about **ARCHITECTURE**, see Chapter 1. See also OC **ARCHITECTURE**, Chapters 1 and 2.

GETTING STARTED

Look at the photo. Discuss the questions with your class.

1. Do you know about solar panels? What do they do? How do they make energy?

2. In what kinds of places do people put solar panels? Give examples. Also give examples of places in your city with solar panels.

⬆ Go to **MyEnglishLab** to complete a self-assessment.

READ

SKILL: SCANNING FOR SPECIFIC INFORMATION

Sometimes you want to find one piece of information in a text. For example, you want to find just a number or a name. So you read quickly, looking for that specific information. This kind of quick reading is called **scanning**. You do not read every word of the text because you do not need to.

Sometimes you scan for the answer to a question. For example, your class is going to read a text about Hawaii. Your teacher asks,

How big is Hawaii?

Before you scan the text for the answer, think of words that can help you find the information, like *miles* and *kilometers*. Numbers might also help. Then quickly scan the text. When you find a number or a word about size, read that sentence. It probably has your answer.

> **CULTURE NOTE**
>
> People in the United States use *miles* (*mi*) to talk about distances. For example, the distance between New York and San Francisco is 2,566 miles. People in most other countries use *kilometers* (*km*). One mile is 1.61 kilometers. So it is about 4,130 km from New York to San Francisco.

Scan this text to answer the question: *How big is Hawaii?*

Hawaii

Hawaii is a group of islands in the middle of the Pacific Ocean. It is one of the 50 states in the United States. The islands cover 11,000 square miles of land. Hawaii has lots of beaches and some really nice mountains.

If you scan for numbers and words about size, you can find the information easily: 11,000 square miles.

When you scan for a piece of information, think of words to look for and then read quickly.

How to Scan

1. Decide what information you need to find.

2. Think of words that can help you find the information you need.

3. Do not read every word. Look for the words related to the information you need.

VOCABULARY PREVIEW

A. Read the sentences. Look at the boldfaced words and phrases. Do you know what they mean? Share your ideas with a partner.

1. There are 98 students in the class. That's **nearly** 100 people!

2. There are five **oceans** in the world: the Pacific, the Atlantic, the Indian, the Southern, and the Arctic Oceans.

3. People often wear **special** clothes to play a sport.

4. In Hawaii, there are really big **waves** in the ocean.

5. That actor is very **famous**. Many people know who he is.

6. There is a party on the **roof** of that apartment building. You can see the people on the top of the building.

7. Hawaii **is made up of** hundreds of islands. There are eight big islands and hundreds of small ones.

8. You need **energy** to make your home warm when it's cold.

B. Write the boldfaced words and phrases from Part A next to their definitions.

_____ 1. describing a person or thing that many people know about

_____ 2. different from other things

_____ 3. power from oil, gas, wind, or the sun, for example

_____ 4. is formed from different parts put together

_____ 5. lines of high water moving across an ocean or sea

_____ 6. close, but not exactly; almost

_____ 7. the top part of a building

_____ 8. very big areas of salt water

An ocean wave

⊘ Go to **MyEnglishLab** to complete a vocabulary practice.

PREDICT

Look at the title of the text and the pictures. Check (✓) the ideas that you think the text will be about.

The text will be about _____ .

☐ a hotel on an island

☐ boats in the ocean

☐ the weather

☐ buildings in a city

READ

A. Read the question before each paragraph. Scan the paragraph to find the answer. Then read the paragraph.

> **GRAMMAR NOTE**
>
> *Maldives* is a plural noun, but it is the name of one country. So, like *the United States*, it takes a singular verb: ***The Maldives is** a small country near India.*

A Modern Hotel in the Maldives

> 1. How many islands are in the Maldives? (Hint: Scan for numbers and the word *islands*.) _____

1 Just south of India, in the Indian Ocean, there is a country called the Maldives. The country is made up of nearly 1,200 islands. About 400,000 people live there, and many more come to visit. Why? The islands are famous for their beautiful beaches, perfect weather, and nice hotels. The Maldives is home to the Finolhu Villas. It's a special hotel on Gasfinolhu Island.

The Maldives has beautiful beaches.

The Maldives is in the Indian Ocean.

(Continued)

2. What is the shape of the ceilings in the Finolhu Villas? (Hint: Look for the word *shape*.) _____

2 Why are the Finolhu Villas so special? First, this hotel is not just one big building with many rooms. The guests at this hotel stay in small buildings called *villas*. The villas are special because they are not on land. They are built over the water. And inside the villas, the ceilings (the walls above the rooms) are special, too. They are not flat. They are in the shape of ocean waves.

3. Where does the hotel get its energy? (Hint: Look for the word *energy*.)

_____

3 The Finolhu Villas are special in another way, too. The hotel gets all of its energy from the sun. You get to the villas from the land by a long walkway. There are solar panels on the roof over the walkway. They make the hotel carbon-neutral.

The long walkway with solar panels at the Finolhu Villas

B. Look at your predictions again. Were they correct?

CULTURE NOTE

There is too much carbon dioxide (CO_2) in the air from burning oil, coal, and gas. Most people want to stop putting CO_2 into the air and make the air cleaner. So they are trying to get CO_2 out of the air (by planting trees, for example). Some people are making buildings that put no more CO_2 into the air than they take out. These buildings are called *carbon neutral*.

⊙ Go to **MyEnglishLab** to reread the text.

READ AGAIN

A. Read the text again. Then complete the sentences.

1. The Maldives is in the _____ Ocean.

2. The Maldives is famous for its beaches, weather, and _____.

3. Guests at the Finolhu Villas stay in villas on _____.

4. The Finolhu Villas get _____ from the sun.

5. The walkways connect _____.

6. The hotel is carbon neutral because of its _____.

B. Read the questions. Discuss them with a partner.

1. Describe the Finolhu Villas. Why is the hotel special?

2. Do you want to go to the Maldives? Why or why not?

C. Read the questions. Discuss them with the class.

1. What do you do when you scan?

2. When is scanning helpful? Give examples of when you scan the text in a book, magazine, or newspaper, and when you scan online. Is scanning easy or difficult?

VOCABULARY REVIEW

Complete the sentences with the words and phrases from the box.

energy	is made up of	ocean	special
famous	nearly	roof	waves

1. I like to go swimming in the _____.

2. That's a very _____ building. Everyone knows it. It's the Eiffel Tower.

3. Each team on the soccer field _____ 11 players.

4. Today is a _____ day—it's my birthday!

5. The children can't swim in the ocean today. The _____ are very big.

6. The _____ of a building keeps out the rain.

7. Mount Everest is 29,029 feet high. It's _____ 30,000 feet.

8. Many homes in this area get _____ from the solar panels on their roofs.

A birthday party

● Go to **MyEnglishLab** to read another text.

Mount Everest

WRITE

SKILL: DESCRIBING OBJECTS

We use our eyes to understand the world. We often talk and write about the people, places, and objects we see. We need to be able to describe them well. It is an important skill for academic writing. Here is some useful vocabulary for describing objects.

SHAPES

This is a **square** clock.

Balls are **round**.

The computer screen is **flat**.

MATERIALS

This is a **glass** table.

There's a **plastic** bottle on the beach.

This is a **metal** chair.

The floor is made of **wood**.

Before you write about an object, take some time to look at it. Think about its location: Where is it? Think about its appearance (what it looks like): What shape, color, material, and size is it?

A. Think about the TV in this photo. Some words to describe the TV are:

on a wall	*big*	*wide*
above a fireplace	*flat*	*black*

B. Read the sentences about the TV. Write three more sentences to describe it.

1. _There is a TV on the wall._

2. _It is black._

3. It is _____.

4. It is _____.

5. _____

REMEMBER

Complete the sentence.

When you describe an object, describe the object's _____ and its _____ .

Grammar for Writing Using adjectives in sentences

Adjectives are words for describing people, places, and things. For example, adjectives can tell the color (*blue, green*), size (*big, small*), and shape (*round, square*) of something.

We use adjectives in sentences in different ways. Study the rules and examples in the chart.

ADJECTIVES

	Rules	Examples
1.	Adjectives can come after the verb *be*.	The car **is black**. The houses **are small**.
2.	Adjectives can come before nouns.	It's a **black car**. I live in a **small house**.
3.	You can connect two adjectives with *and*.	My phone is **small and black**. I like **warm and sunny** weather.

GRAMMAR NOTE

Nouns are words for people (for example, *John, teacher*), places (*New York, school*), things (*chair, window*), and concepts or ideas (*education, love*).

GRAMMAR NOTE

Remember to use the correct forms of the verb *be*. The form depends on the subject.

Subject	Be	
I	**am**	in class
He / She / It	**is**	cold.
You / We / They	**are**	ready.

REMEMBER

Complete the sentence.

Adjectives are words for _____ people, places, and things.

A. Read the description. Underline the six adjectives.

The Empire State Building is in New York City. It is a skyscraper (a very tall building) with 102 stories (floors). For skyscrapers, the building is old. It was built in 1931. Many people think that it is a nice building because of its lights. At night, the building's lights can be many colors—sometimes they are white, and other times they are red and blue.

B. Put the words in the correct order. Write sentences.

1. lives / apartment / big / in / Maria / a

   Maria lives in a big apartment.

2. nice / a / it / apartment / is

   _____

3. building / in / modern / Maria's apartment / a / is

   _____

4. the architect / famous / is / of the building

   _____

5. the building / roof / a / has / black

   _____

6. tall / wide / windows / are / the / and

   _____

7. park / a / there's / next to the building / beautiful

   _____

C. Write about an object in the classroom.

1. Find an object in the room. Write three sentences with adjectives to describe it. Do not use the name of the object in your sentences.

2. Work with a partner. Share your sentences. Guess the object that your partner's sentences describe.

3. Choose different objects to write about, and guess again.

⊙ Go to **MyEnglishLab** for more grammar practice.

WRITE DESCRIPTIONS OF OBJECTS
STEP 1: READ TO WRITE

A. Read the words and definitions. You will see these words in the text.

Glossary

are made of: are built from (a material)

cover: be on every part of the top of something

light: energy from the sun

protect: keep something safe

section: a part of something

B. Read each paragraph. Then circle the correct answer to complete the sentence.

Solar Panels

1 You can see big solar panels in many places. They are usually black or blue. Sometimes they cover the roofs of homes or office buildings. Sometimes they stand in fields or other open spaces. In countries with deserts, like Mexico and Egypt, there are thousands of solar panels in the middle of the desert.

> 1. Paragraph 1 describes places with _____ .
>   a. homes   b. solar panels

2 Solar panels usually have many sections. Each section is called a module. For homes, modules are usually 65 x 39 inches (165 x 99 centimeters). The modules have many smaller parts. These are called photovoltaic (PV) cells. There are usually 60 cells in a module: ten rows with six cells in each row.

> 2. Paragraph 2 is about the _____ of solar panels.
>   a. sections and modules   b. rows and homes

3 PV cells are small flat squares. They are mostly made of silicon. They have a few thin layers on top of each other, like pages in a book. The top layer is glass. It protects the cell. There are two layers of electrodes: one under the glass and one at the bottom of the cell. Between the electrodes are semiconductors. The semiconductors and electrodes take light and make electricity.

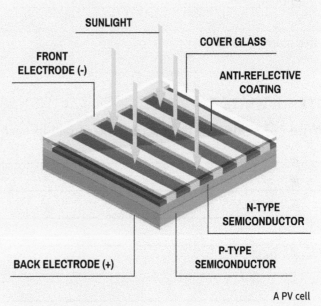

SUNLIGHT

COVER GLASS

FRONT ELECTRODE (-)

ANTI-REFLECTIVE COATING

N-TYPE SEMICONDUCTOR

P-TYPE SEMICONDUCTOR

BACK ELECTRODE (+)

A PV cell

> 3. Paragraph 3 is about the _____ of PV cells.
>   a. layers   b. silicon

C. Complete the chart with adjectives from the text.

Color	Size	Shape

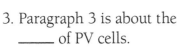 Go to **MyEnglishLab** to reread the text.

STEP 2: PREPARE TO WRITE

Work with a partner. Look at the photos. In the chart, write adjectives that describe each object.

Object	Color	Size	Shape	Material
the chair				
the house				
the alarm clock				

STEP 3: WRITE

Write 2–3 sentences to describe the object in each picture in Step 2.

_____

_____

_____

_____

_____

_____

_____

_____

STEP 4: PROOFREAD AND EDIT

A. Proofread your sentences.

- Do you use adjectives correctly?

- Are there any spelling mistakes?

- Does every sentence begin with a capital letter and end with a period?

B. Work with a partner. Share your sentences. Answer the questions in the Peer Review Form. Share your answers with your partner. Ask your partner about your sentences. Then edit them.

Peer Review Form	Yes	No
1. Does your partner write about the things in the three pictures?	☐	☐
2. Are the descriptions correct?	☐	☐
3. Does your partner use adjectives correctly?	☐	☐
4. Are there any spelling mistakes? If there are, circle them.	☐	☐

C. Read the questions. Discuss them with the class.

1. Is it easy to describe objects? Explain.

2. What should you think about when you describe objects?

BUILDING VOCABULARY

UNDERSTANDING SYNONYMS AND ANTONYMS

Some pairs of words have similar meanings, like the verbs *begin* and *start*. These are called **synonyms**. Other pairs have opposite meanings, like *begin* and *end*. These are called **antonyms**. Learning synonyms and antonyms together can help you to learn new words.

Look at the adjective synonyms and antonyms in the chart.

Adjectives		
	Synonyms	Antonyms
tall	high	low / short
thin	skinny	thick / fat
fast	quick	slow

It is important to remember that synonyms do not always have exactly the same meaning. So sometimes we cannot replace a word with a synonym. For example, we can ask either *How **tall** is the Eiffel Tower?* or *How **high** is the Eiffel Tower?* But we can use only *tall* in the question *How **tall** is the woman.* We cannot replace *tall* with *high* because we do not use *high* to describe a person's height.

> **TIP**
>
> To learn more synonyms and build your vocabulary, use a thesaurus. A thesaurus is like a dictionary, but, instead of meanings, it has synonyms.

A. Read the pairs of sentences. One sentence has a synonym for a word that you know. The other sentence has an antonym. Write the synonyms and antonyms on the lines.

1. *beautiful*

   a. The mountains are **gorgeous**. They are really beautiful at this time of year.

   b. That's a very **ugly** building. I hate looking at it.

   A synonym of *beautiful*: _____

   An antonym of *beautiful*: _____

2. *big*

   a. The Burj Khalifa in Dubai is **huge**! It's the biggest building in the world.

   b. These chairs are **tiny**. How can anybody sit in them? They're so small!

   A synonym of *big*: _____

   An antonym of *big*: _____

3. *famous*

   a. New York is a **well-known** city. Millions of tourists visit it each year.

   b. Burlington, Vermont, is nearly **unknown**. It is a small city in the United States with few visitors.

   A synonym of *famous*: _____

   An antonym of *famous*: _____

4. *old*

   a. Have you seen the author's most **recent** book? It's very new.

   b. The museum has many **ancient** works of art. Most are over 2,000 years old.

   A synonym of *old*: _____

   An antonym of *old*: _____

   > **VOCABULARY NOTE**
   >
   > We often use *ancient* for buildings and objects that people made a very long time ago. Do not use *ancient* to describe people.

5. *special*

   a. That's quite an **ordinary** building. It looks like most other buildings in the city.

   b. Frank Gehry's architecture is **unique**. His buildings are always very different from the buildings nearby.

   A synonym of *special*: _____

   An antonym of *special*: _____

The Guggenheim Museum in Bilbao: Frank Gehry, architect

B. Look at the photos. Circle the correct words to complete the sentences.

1. The building in the photo is just **unique / ordinary**. There's nothing special about it, is there?

2. I love the New York City skyline! It's **gorgeous / ugly** at night.

3. This memory card is **huge / tiny**.

4. The Coliseum is one of the many **ancient / recent** buildings in Rome.

5. The Eiffel Tower is one of the most **well-known / unknown** works of architecture in the world.

6. The little tugboat is guiding the **huge / tiny** ship.

7. One **unique / ordinary** building in Prague is the Dancing House. I don't know of any other building like it.

C. Look at the list of buildings and objects below. Use your phone or computer to find a photo as an example of each one. Write the names of the buildings or objects on the lines. Then share your photos with a small group. Explain why you chose them. Discuss everyone's choices.

1. A unique building in China _____

2. A huge statue of a person _____

3. A well-known work of art _____

4. An ancient building _____

5. A gorgeous bridge or skyline _____

6. An ugly building or other work of architecture _____

⬆ Go to **MyEnglishLab** to complete a vocabulary practice.

APPLY YOUR SKILLS

In this chapter, you read about the Finolhu Villas, a unique hotel in the Maldives. You also read about solar panels. In Apply Your Skills, you will learn about Apple Park, a modern building in the United States. Then you will write sentences describing a building of your choice.

VOCABULARY PREVIEW

A. Read the sentences. Look at the boldfaced words and phrases. Do you know what they mean? Share your ideas with a partner.

1. Modern life is easier because of science and **technology**.

2. The Finolhu Villas **are located** in the Maldives.

3. There are big windows on the front, back, and **sides** of the building.

4. People like parks and other **green spaces** in their cities.

5. Water **surrounds** islands.

6. I'm tired. I need to **rest**.

7. In my house, there are three bedrooms **in total**—one on the first floor and two on the second floor.

8. Palm Jumeirah **looks like** a palm tree.

> **VOCABULARY NOTE**
>
> *Tech* is a short form of *technology*. You will often see *tech* used as an adjective before a noun, as in *tech company*. *Tech* can also be a noun, as in *The phone has all the newest tech.*

B. Write the boldfaced words and phrases from Part A next to their definitions.

_____ 1. when all the things are added together

_____ 2. sit or lie down to relax

_____ 3. the parts of something that are not the top, bottom, front, or back

_____ 4. modern machines or ways of doing things developed by science

_____ 5. are in a place

_____ 6. is completely around something

_____ 7. areas with a lot of trees and plants, like parks

_____ 8. is similar in appearance

🔊 Go to **MyEnglishLab** to complete a vocabulary practice.

PREDICT

Look at the title of the text and photos on page 39. Do you agree with the predictions below? Circle *Yes* or *No*.

1. This text will be about a building where people sell apples. Yes / No

2. This text will describe a modern building. Yes / No

READ

A. Read the question before each paragraph. Scan the paragraph to find the answer. Then read the paragraph.

Apple's Modern Building

1. How many people work at Apple Park? _____

1 Apple Park is the home of Apple Inc., the famous company for computer technology. It is located near San Francisco, California. It is in Silicon Valley (the world's center for computer technology). Apple Park is close to other big tech companies, such as Facebook™ and Alphabet™, the parent company of Google™. About 12,000 people work in this modern building.

2. How tall are the windows of Apple Park? _____

2 Apple Park sits on 175 acres (71 hectares) of land in the city of Cupertino. The building is a circle. It is 1 mile across. It has 2.8 million square feet of space inside—more than 50 soccer fields. It has four floors above ground and more below ground. The sides of the building are made of 45-foot tall windows.

3. How many trees does Apple Park have in its green spaces? _____

3 Green space surrounds the building. There is also a green space inside the circle. It is a park with trees, gardens, walkways, and places to rest. In total, there are more than 7,000 trees in Apple Park.

4. How does the building get most of its energy? _____

4 From above, Apple Park looks like a spaceship. That is because of two things: its shape and the solar panels that cover the roof. The roof looks like it is metal. The panels can make 75 percent of the energy the building needs.

B. Look at your predictions again. Were they correct?

🔵 Go to **MyEnglishLab** to reread the text.

CULTURE NOTE

Many countries measure land in acres. An acre is often a square with sides of 208.71 feet (63.61 meters). A hectare has four sides of 100 meters.

READ AGAIN

A. Read the text again. Then complete the sentences.

1. Apple Park is located near other _____ companies.

2. Apple Park has the shape of a _____ .

3. There are four _____ above ground.

4. The sides of the building are made of _____ .

5. Inside and outside the circle of the building, there are _____ spaces.

6. On the roof, there are _____ .

B. Complete the sentences about the topic of each paragraph. Write the letters.

_____ 1. Paragraph 1 describes …   a. the roof of Apple Park.

_____ 2. Paragraph 2 describes …   b. the Apple Park building.

_____ 3. Paragraph 3 describes …   c. Apple Park's location.

_____ 4. Paragraph 4 describes …   d. Apple Park's green spaces.

C. Read the questions. Discuss them in a small group.

1. Apple Park is an office building. Why do you think they use the word *park* in its name?

2. Would you like to work at a place like Apple Park? Why or why not?

3. Do the photos of Apple Park help you to understand the text? How?

VOCABULARY REVIEW

Complete the sentences with the words and phrases from the box.

green spaces	is located	rest	surround
In total	looks like	side	technology (tech)

1. There are 12,000 workers _____ at Apple Park.

2. After I work hard, I like to have a _____ .

3. Trees _____ the house, so you only see green when you look out the windows.

4. The Burj Khalifa _____ in Dubai.

5. Microsoft and Samsung are big _____ companies.

6. Apple Park _____ a spaceship.

7. There are no windows on the south _____ of the building.

8. _____ are good places for exercise.

THINK VISUALLY

Work with a partner. Look at the photos of buildings from different parts of the world. Take turns describing the buildings. Try to describe each building's location, size, age, colors, and other features (for example, its roof, windows, or doors).

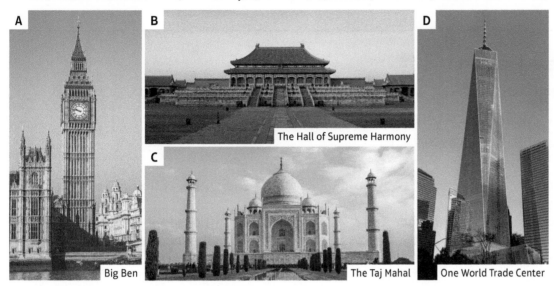

A

B

The Hall of Supreme Harmony

D

C

Big Ben

The Taj Mahal

One World Trade Center

GRAMMAR

USING ADJECTIVES IN SENTENCES

Read the paragraph. Correct the five mistakes.

Michael lives in Somerville, Massachusetts. It is a city small in the United States. He has a house there. It is blue, white. It has many windows. Like a lot of houses, it has a roof black. Inside, on the first floor, there is a kitchen nice. In the kitchen, there is a big table with chairs. The chairs are white black. It is his favorite room in the house because he loves to cook.

ASSIGNMENT

Write sentences to describe a building.

PREPARE TO WRITE

Work with a partner. Think of a building to write about. Find a photo of it. Make a list of words to describe the building.

Location: _____   Shape: _____

Color: _____   Other: _____

Size: _____

WRITE

Write five or more sentences about the building. Remember to write about the location.

_____

_____

_____

_____

_____

PROOFREAD AND EDIT

A. Proofread your sentences.

- Do you write about a building? Do you write about its location?
- Do you use adjectives correctly?
- Are there any spelling mistakes?
- Does every sentence begin with a capital letter and end with a period?

B. Work with a partner. Share your sentences. Answer the questions in the Peer Review Form. Share your answers with your partner. Ask your partner about your sentences. Then edit them.

Peer Review Form	Yes	No
1. Does your partner describe a building?	☐	☐
2. Does your partner write about its location?	☐	☐
3. Does your partner use adjectives to describe the building?	☐	☐
4. Is the grammar correct?	☐	☐
5. Are there any spelling mistakes? If there are, circle them.	☐	☐

⬆ Go to **MyEnglishLab** to complete grammar and vocabulary practices.

DEVELOP SOFT SKILLS

USING GRAPHIC ORGANIZERS TO STUDY VOCABULARY

In your English class, you are learning many new words. In any language class, learning vocabulary is very important! It's important in other university courses, too. In science classes, you need to learn the language of biology or chemistry, for example. What can you do to understand and remember everything? Graphic organizers are a great tool for organizing new vocabulary and ideas.

A. Read the words and definitions. You will see these words in the text on the next page.

> **Glossary**
>
> **category:** a group of things that are the same in some way
>
> **column:** a tall narrow space in a chart
>
> **researcher:** a person who studies something to find out new facts about it
>
> **topic:** something you talk, read, or write about
>
> **wide:** large from side to side

B. Read the text.

Organizing Your Vocabulary and Ideas

Vocabulary Charts

1 Charts are good for putting information into categories. For example, you can make a chart that has columns for different types of words:
- Nouns – words that name people, places, things, ideas
- Verbs – words for actions or states of being
- Adjectives – words that describe people, places, things, ideas

Nouns	Verbs	Adjectives	other
beach	connect	ancient	below
roof	be made up of	famous	on top of
scientist		gorgeous	to the left/right of
		well-known	

DATE:

2 This chart has some of the vocabulary you studied in Unit 1. In the "other" column are words and phrases that aren't nouns, verbs, or adjectives.

3 Some students like to make vocabulary charts on their computers. Others like to make their charts in a notebook. Researchers say that writing information with a pen helps us remember it better than writing it on a computer.

Mind Maps

4 A mind map is a way to take notes. It's a way to take information that you hear or read, think about it, and organize it as you like. Mind maps can help you understand, study, and remember new words. Here is an example of a mind map showing some Unit 1 vocabulary.

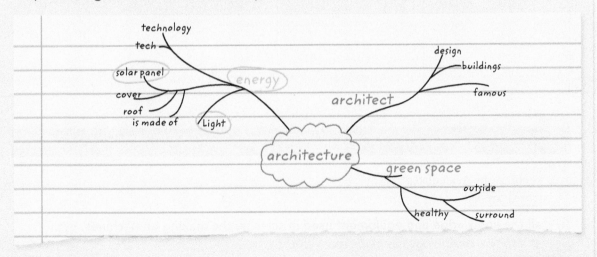

(Continued)

5 How do you make a mind map? Take a piece of paper. Turn it so it is wide, not tall. Start by drawing a cloud in the center of the paper. Put your topic there. Draw lines out from this cloud. These are branches (like the branches of a tree). On the branches, write words and phrases that connect to the topic. You can use color to make your mind map more interesting to look at. Color will help you remember, too.

C. Complete the sentences with the words from the box.

chart	color	columns	organize	remember	topic

1. You can use a _____ to organize words into categories or groups.

2. You can make a vocabulary chart with _____ for nouns, verbs, adjectives, and other types of words or phrases.

3. Writing words with a pen can help you _____ them.

4. When you make a mind map, you can _____ the information as you like.

5. Put the _____ of your mind map in the middle of your paper.

6. Use _____ for your mind map to make it interesting and help you remember the words.

D. Work with a partner. Discuss the words in the box and add them to the chart. Use your dictionary if you do not know which column a word should go in. For an example, see the dictionary entry below for the noun *technology*.

be located	look like	ocean	surround	tiny
energy	nearly	special	technology	unique

Nouns	Verbs	Adjectives	Other

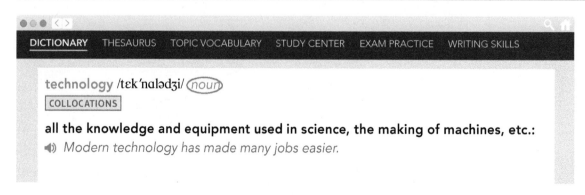

DICTIONARY   THESAURUS   TOPIC VOCABULARY   STUDY CENTER   EXAM PRACTICE   WRITING SKILLS

technology /tɛkˈnɑlədʒi/ *noun*

COLLOCATIONS

all the knowledge and equipment used in science, the making of machines, etc.:
◄) *Modern technology has made many jobs easier.*

E. Make a mind map in the space below. Use *building* as your topic. Draw branches and add words from Unit 1 or any other words you know that connect to the topic.

WHAT DID YOU LEARN?

Check (✓) the skills and vocabulary you learned. Circle the things you need to practice.

SKILLS

☐ I can scan a reading for specific information.

☐ I can describe objects.

☐ I can use adjectives in sentences.

☐ I can understand synonyms and antonyms.

☐ I can use graphic organizers to study vocabulary.

VOCABULARY

☐ ancient	☐ look like	☐ surround
☐ be located	☐ nearly	☐ technology (tech)
☐ be made up of	☐ ocean	☐ tiny
☐ energy	☐ ordinary	☐ ugly
☐ famous	☐ recent	☐ unique
☐ green space	☐ rest	☐ unknown
☐ gorgeous	☐ roof	☐ wave
☐ huge	☐ side	☐ well-known
☐ in total	☐ special	

◐ Go to **MyEnglishLab** to complete a self-assessment.

◐ Go to **MyEnglishLab** for a challenge reading about Architecture.

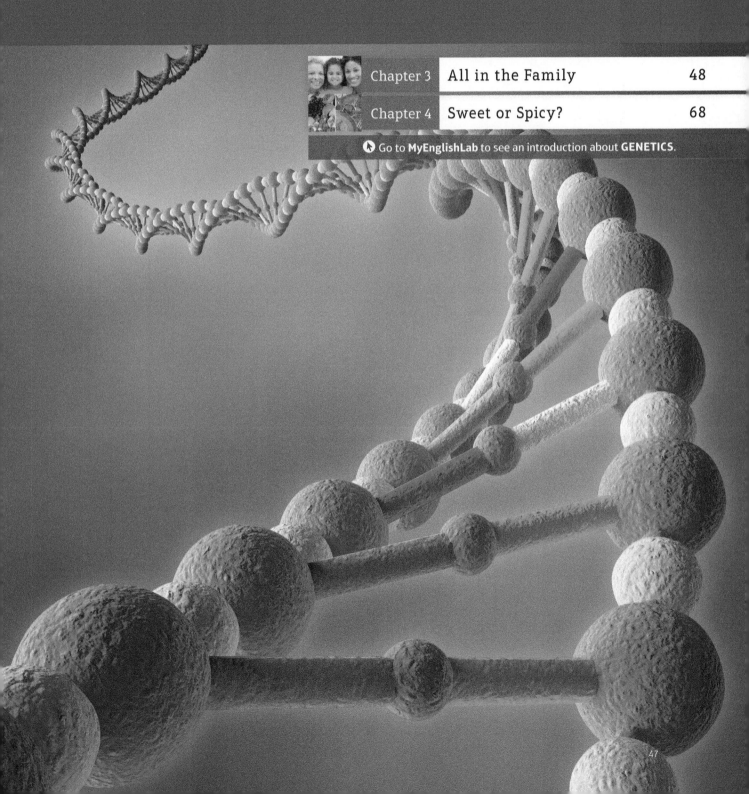

Genetics

Go to **MyEnglishLab** to see an introduction about **GENETICS**.

Chapter 3 All in the Family

CHAPTER PROFILE

Genetics is about the DNA of all living things: people, animals, and plants. The study of genetics includes studying the relationship between DNA and how people look.

This chapter is about how people's genes affect the way they look.

You will read about

• a person's genes and appearance.

• two friends who look different because of their genes.

• how the environment can affect the genes and color of an animal.

You will write a description of a friend or family member.

OUTCOMES

• Identify the topic and main idea of a text

• Describe a person's appearance

• Use *have* and *be* in descriptions

• Describe physical appearance

• Work in groups

For more about **GENETICS**, see Chapter 4. See also [OC] **GENETICS**, Chapters 3 and 4.

GETTING STARTED

Work with a partner. Look at the photo on page 48 and answer the questions.

1. Do you think the three people in the photo are in the same family? Explain your answer.

2. Do you look like someone in your family?

🕐 Go to **MyEnglishLab** to complete a self-assessment.

READ

SKILL: IDENTIFYING THE TOPIC AND MAIN IDEA OF A TEXT

A reader's first question about a text is usually, "What's it about?" The answer is the **topic** of the text. The topic is the person, place, thing, or idea that the writer is talking about.

The **main idea** of the text is the writer's most important idea about the topic. It is the idea that the writer wants you to understand and remember the most. In many texts, each paragraph has a main idea. Together, the main ideas of the paragraphs make the main idea of the whole text.

You can often find the main idea of a paragraph in the first sentence. Writers often state their main point there. In the other sentences, writers then use **details** to support, or explain, the main point. Sometimes writers return to the main idea in the last sentence of the paragraph. Read this paragraph.

> We are often very similar to our parents. Short parents usually have short children. Tall parents usually have tall children. Smart people? They usually have smart children. This is because we get our genes from our parents. Because of genes, we often grow up to be like our parents.

Father and son

You can see that the main idea of the paragraph is similar to the first sentence: *We are often very similar to our parents.* The other sentences in the paragraph give examples and explain the main idea in more detail.

REMEMBER

Complete the sentences.

The _____ of a text is the person, place, or thing the writer is talking about.

The _____ of a text is the writer's most important idea about the topic.

TIP

If you see a word that you do not know, wait before going to a dictionary. First, use the **context** to try to guess the meaning. *The context of a word* means the words and sentences that come before and after it.

Study the context of the word you do not know. Try to understand the sentence. Then make a guess about the word's meaning. After you finish reading, use a dictionary to check the meaning of the word.

VOCABULARY PREVIEW

A. Read the sentences. Look at the boldfaced words. Do you know what they mean? Share your ideas with a partner.

1. My brother and I look **alike**. We have the same hair color and eye color, and our noses are the same shape.

2. Your height, size, hair, and eye color are all parts of your **appearance**, or the way you look.

3. There are 16 people in the class. **Half** are men, and the other eight are women.

4. There is a **pair** of shoes by the door. Both shoes are a little dirty.

5. Many people living in wet places eat **rice** because it grows easily there.

6. London and New York are **similar**: They are big cities and they have a lot of people from other countries.

B. Write the words from Part A next to their definitions.

_____ 1. two things of the same kind that go together

_____ 2. the way a person looks to other people

_____ 3. one of two equal parts of something

_____ 4. nearly the same, but different in very small ways

_____ 5. in the same way or in almost the same way

_____ 6. a food that is usually white, comes from a plant, and is often eaten in Asia

○ Go to **MyEnglishLab** to complete a vocabulary practice.

PREDICT

Look at the title of the text and the pictures on page 51. What do you think the text will be about? Circle *Yes* or *No.*

1. What people look like   Yes / No

2. The different foods that people like   Yes / No

3. Relationships between parents and children   Yes / No

READ

A. Read the text and answer the question after each paragraph.

Why Do We Look Like Our Parents?

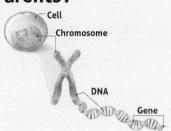

1 My father and I look alike. He's tall, and I'm tall. His hair is brown, and my hair is brown. We both have blue eyes. It is not unusual for a father and child to look alike. Billions of people around the world look just like their parents. Why? It is because of our genes, the pieces of DNA found in our cells.

1. What is the main idea of Paragraph 1?
   a. Parents and children often look alike.
   b. Genes give us our hair color.

2 Genes have all the information that makes us look the way we do. This information is like a long list of instructions. It tells our bodies how to make our eyes, ears, arms, legs, and all the other parts of our bodies. Our genes come in pairs: One gene in each pair comes from our mother, and the other gene comes from our father. So I have a lot of the same information, from the same genes, as my father. And that information makes my eyes and hair look like his.

2. What is the main idea of Paragraph 2?
   a. We get half our genes from each parent.
   b. Genes have a lot of information about our looks.

3 All living things have genes. People have about 20,000 genes. Cats and dogs have about the same number as we do. Some plants have many more. For example, a tomato has nearly 32,000 genes, and rice has more than 50,000. Plants and animals also get their genes from their parents. So they, too, will be similar in appearance to their parents.

Tomatoes have nearly 32,000 genes.

3. What is the main idea of Paragraph 3?
   a. Genes are in all people, plants, and animals.
   b. Rice and tomatoes have more genes than people.

B. Look at your predictions again. Were they correct?

○ Go to **MyEnglishLab** to reread the text.

READ AGAIN

A. Read the text again. Then read the statements below. Circle *T* (true) or *F* (false).

T / F   1. Few people look like their parents.

T / F   2. DNA is in our cells.

T / F   3. We have pairs of genes.

T / F   4. People have 30,000 genes.

T / F   5. Cats have many more genes than dogs.

T / F   6. Rice has more than 50,000 genes.

T / F   7. Only animals get their genes from their parents.

B. Work with a partner. Compare your answers in Part A. Correct the false statements.

C. Answer Question 1. Then work with a partner or in a small group. Discuss your answers to all three questions.

1. What do you look like? Circle your answers.

   I am **short / average height / tall.**

   I have **brown / blue / green / gray** eyes.

   I have **black / brown / blond / _____** hair.

_{other}

   I have **straight / wavy / curly** hair.

Straight hair

Wavy hair

Curly hair

2. Do you look like your mother or father? Do you look like both of them? Explain.

3. When you are looking for the main idea of a paragraph, in which sentence can you often find it?

VOCABULARY REVIEW

Complete the sentences with the words from the box.

alike	appearance	half	pair	rice	similar

1. Some people eat _____ every day.

2. Tomatoes and apples have _____ colors and shapes, but they are very different.

3. My two sisters look _____. They both have curly brown hair, blue eyes, and nice smiles.

4. I need to buy a new _____ of shoes.

5. Your _____ is important. It's the first thing that people see when they meet you.

6. _____ an hour is 30 minutes.

⬤ Go to **MyEnglishLab** to read another text.

WRITE

SKILL: DESCRIBING A PERSON'S APPEARANCE

People love to talk about other people. We like to write about other people, too. An important part in writing about people is to describe their **physical appearance**, or what they look like.

In English-speaking countries, we focus on a few things when we describe a person's appearance: his or her age, height (how tall he or she is), hair, and eye color.

Look at the photo of Cynthia (she's on the left) and read the sentences.

Cynthia is young.

She is short.

She has long, straight, dark hair.

You can also describe other parts of a person's appearance, especially if they are unusual or special. Look at the photo of Michael and read the sentences.

Michael has a nice smile.

He has beautiful teeth.

REMEMBER

Complete the sentences.

When describing a person's appearance, write about his or her age, height, _____, and _____. Also, write about other things that are _____, like a nice smile.

Grammar for Writing Using *have* and *be* in descriptions

There are many ways to use the verb **have**. You can use it to say that a person owns something:

> I **have** a red car.

> Steve **has** a lot of money.

You can also use *have* to describe a person's appearance:

> She **has** brown eyes.

> Ray **has** long hair.

In a sentence with *have* for describing a person's appearance, the subject is always the person.

DESCRIPTIONS WITH *HAVE*

Subject (a person)	*Have (+ Not)*	Object
I You We They Paula and Aaron	**have** **don't have**	curly hair. perfect teeth. big feet. glasses.
Tim Christen He She	**has** **doesn't have**	

> **GRAMMAR NOTE**
>
> We use the verb *be* to give someone's age.
> *I **am** 35 years old.*
> *She **is** 22.*
> *My parents **are** in their sixties.*

You can use the verb **be** in a description of a person, too. The subject of *be* can be the person or a part of the body.

DESCRIPTIONS WITH *BE*

	Subject	Be (+ Not)	Adjective
Subject = a person	I	**am**	short.
	You	**are**	thin.
	Anna	**isn't**	tall.
Subject = a part of the body	My hair	**is**	curly.
	His eyes	**are**	beautiful.
	Your ears	**aren't**	big.

REMEMBER

Complete the sentences with *be* and *have*.

Use the verb _____ + an adjective (like *short*). Use the verb _____ + an object (like *short hair*).

A. Use the correct form of *be (not)* or *have (not)* to complete the sentences.

1. Sami's hair _____ long, but mine is short.

2. Her eyes _____ brown, but his eyes are blue.

3. Danny _____ green eyes, and his mother does, too.

4. I have a small nose. I _____ a big nose.

5. They _____ short hair. They don't like long hair.

6. My hair _____ brown, but my brother's is black.

7. Alex and her brother _____ beautiful eyes.

8. Ahmed is short. He _____ tall.

B. Circle all the words and phrases you can use to complete each sentence.

1. Fatima is _____.
   a. tall
   b. long
   c. 19 years old

2. My brother doesn't have _____.
   a. short
   b. curly hair
   c. big feet

3. Your sisters are _____.
   a. average height
   b. brown eyes
   c. beautiful

4. Vanessa's hair is _____.
   a. short
   b. brown
   c. straight

5. Jin-young has _____.
   a. brown eyes
   b. 31 years old
   c. a nice smile

6. Brian is _____.
   a. blue eyes
   b. long hair
   c. in his thirties

C. Read the paragraph. Correct the five mistakes.

Marcia has two brothers, Jacob and Kevin. Jacob is tall, and he is green eyes. His hair has brown and curly. He also has very big feet. Kevin has short. His eyes are brown, and he is straight, brown hair. Like his sister, he is a beautiful smile.

↻ **Go to MyEnglishLab for more grammar practice.**

WRITE A DESCRIPTION OF A PERSON
STEP 1: READ TO WRITE

A. Read the words and definitions. You will see these words in the text.

> **Glossary**
>
> **difference:** a way that two people or things are not alike
> **percent:** the part (%) out of 100
> **rare:** not often seen or happening
> **several:** more than a few but not many

B. Read the text. Follow the instructions after each paragraph.

Jen and Kris

1 Jen and Kris are friends, and they are similar in some ways. They both come from New York. They are both 20 years old and are studying to be doctors. They like the same TV shows and the same kinds of food. And just like their parents, both Jen and Kris are thin. But of course, there are also differences between them.

> 1. Underline the sentence in Paragraph 1 that describes what Jen and Kris look like.

2 Jen and Kris look different in several ways. Jen is short. She's about five feet three inches tall (160 cm). She has dark, wavy hair, and her eyes are brown. She wears glasses. Kris is tall at five foot eight (173 cm). Her hair is straight and red, and she has blue eyes, just like her parents. She also has freckles.

> 2. Underline the sentences in Paragraph 2 that describe Jen's and Kris's appearance.

3 Genes are a big reason that Jen and Kris are different heights. Jen's parents are short, but Kris's parents are tall. Like most Americans, Jen and Kris are similar to their parents in height. Between 50 and 80 percent of height differences are because of genes.

> 3. Underline the sentence in Paragraph 3 that describes Jen's and Kris's parents.

4 As for Jen's and Kris's hair and eyes, genes are the reason for those differences, too. Different genes make different kinds of melanin. Melanin makes the different colors of our hair, eyes, and skin. Kris's genes are rare: Only about 8 percent of people have blue eyes, and less than 2 percent have red hair. Freckles are genetic, too. Kris's freckles are just like her father's.

4. Underline the sentence in Paragraph 4 that reports facts about blue eyes and red hair.

◑ Go to **MyEnglishLab** to reread the text.

STEP 2: PREPARE TO WRITE

Work with a partner. Look at the photo. Write some words to describe the man.

1. age: _young_____

2. hair: _____

3. hair color: _____

4. eyes: _____

5. other: _____

STEP 3: WRITE

Write five or more sentences to describe the man in the photo. Use *have (not)* and *be (not)* in your sentences.

_____

_____

_____

_____

_____

_____

_____

STEP 4: PROOFREAD AND EDIT

A. Proofread your sentences.

- Do you use the verbs *have* and *be* correctly?

- Are there any spelling mistakes?

- Does every sentence begin with a capital letter and end with a period?

B. Work with a partner. Share your sentences. Answer the questions in the Peer Review Form. Share your answers with your partner. Ask your partner about your sentences. Then edit them.

Peer Review Form	Yes	No
1. Does your partner write about the man's appearance?	☐	☐
2. Is the description correct?	☐	☐
3. Does your partner use *have* and *be* correctly?	☐	☐
4. Are there any spelling mistakes? If there are, circle them.	☐	☐

C. Read the questions. Discuss them with a partner.

1. What do you write about when you describe a person's appearance?

2. Do you like to write descriptions of people? Is it easy to do? Why or why not?

BUILDING VOCABULARY

DESCRIBING PHYSICAL APPEARANCE

There are many words to describe a person's appearance. Some, like *pretty*, *handsome*, and *good-looking*, describe people that we think are nice to look at. *Pretty* is used for women and girls only, and *handsome* is used for men. *Cute* is usually used for children.

I think she's **pretty**.

He has **a mustache**.

They're **cute**.

He has **a beard**.

I think he's **handsome**.

They're **good-looking**.

CULTURE NOTE

In many English-speaking countries, it is not nice to talk about a person's weight. Never use *fat* to describe someone.

A. Match the words with their uses.

_____ 1. mustache

_____ 2. beard

_____ 3. handsome

_____ 4. pretty

_____ 5. cute

_____ 6. good-looking

a. usually describes children

b. usually describes a woman

c. usually describes a man

d. can describe men or women

e. hair over the lower part of a man's face

f. hair above a man's mouth

B. Look at the photos and descriptions. There are four mistakes. Correct the mistakes.

1. This is David. Many people think that he's pretty.

   David has short hair. He doesn't have a beard.

2. This is Jillian. She's with her students. Many people think that Jillian is handsome and her students are good-looking.

C. Look at the tasks below. Find your photos and prepare your descriptions. Then work in a small group.

1. Find a photo of a famous woman that you think is pretty. Describe her to your group. Then show them the photo. Ask your group if they think the woman is pretty.

2. Find a photo of a famous man that you think is handsome. Describe him to your group. Then show them the photo. Ask your group if they think the man is handsome.

3. Find a photo of a famous man with a beard or mustache. Describe him to your group. Then show them the photo. Ask your group if they think the man is good-looking.

⬆ Go to **MyEnglishLab** to complete a vocabulary practice.

APPLY YOUR SKILLS

In this chapter, you read about genes, where we get them, and how they affect our appearance. You also read some descriptions of people and how the way they look depends on genetics. In Apply Your Skills, you will read about how the environment can also affect the way both people and animals look.

VOCABULARY PREVIEW

A. Read the sentences. Look at the boldfaced words and phrases. Do you know what they mean? Share your ideas with a partner.

1. Rain **affects** the health of plants.

2. May 8 is my birthday! I **was born** on May 8, 1983.

3. Our classroom has a good **environment** for learning.

4. The cat's **fur** is black.

5. My daughter wants to be a doctor when she **grows up**.

6. In North America, it's **normally** colder in the winter than in the summer.

7. The weather today is **warm**. It's a perfect day to be outside.

B. Write the words and phrases from Part A next to their definitions.

_____ 1. usually

_____ 2. for an animal: came out of the mother's body

_____ 3. a little hot

_____ 4. changes from a child to an adult

_____ 5. the hair on some animals' bodies

_____ 6. the people and things around you that affect you

_____ 7. makes something change or become different

🔊 Go to **MyEnglishLab** to complete a vocabulary practice.

PREDICT

Look at the title of the text below and the photo on page 61. Make two predictions about the text.

1. The reading is about _____ .

2. _____

READ

A. Read the text. Complete the sentence after each paragraph.

The Environment Affects Appearance, Too

1 We know that genes affect how we look. They affect our eye color, height, and hair, for example. Genes don't do this only in people. They also affect the appearance of animals and plants.

1. The main idea of the paragraph is that genes affect how _____ .
   a. people, animals, and plants look
   b. animals and plants look

2 The environment can affect how we look, too. That is because it can affect how genes work. A good example of this is an animal—the Himalayan rabbit. Normally, this rabbit lives in cold places. In a cold environment, it has mostly white fur, but its feet, face, and ears have black fur. As in people, the genes and melanin in the rabbit make the different colors of hair. But when Himalayan rabbits are born and live in warm places (above 30°C), they grow up to be *all* white, with no black fur at all.

2. The main idea of the paragraph is that _____ .
   a. the Himalayan rabbit has white fur
   b. the environment can change how genes work

3 Why are the Himalayan rabbits' feet, face, and ears white in warm environments? It is because the warm weather affects the genes in the cells of these body parts. In warm weather, these cells make a different melanin. It is the same melanin as in the parts of the rabbit's body with white fur. So the rabbit's fur is all white.

3. The main idea of the paragraph is that _____ .
   a. a warm environment affects the Himalayan rabbit's genes for hair color
   b. Himalayan rabbits prefer warm environments

4 The Himalayan rabbit is one example of how the environment can affect appearance. This example shows how an animal's genes can be affected by the world around it. Similar things can happen to the genes of plants and people. So our environment can affect how we look, too.

4. The main idea of the paragraph is that _____ .
   a. genes control how we look
   b. the environment can affect the genes that control appearance

B. Look at your predictions again. Were they correct?

○ Go to **MyEnglishLab** to reread the text.

READ AGAIN

A. Read the text again. Then read the statements below. Circle _T_ (true) or _F_ (false).

T / F   1. All living things have genes.

T / F   2. The Himalayan rabbit usually lives in warm places.

T / F   3. The Himalayan rabbit normally has black fur only on its face and ears.

T / F   4. Himalayan rabbits are all white in places above 30°C.

T / F   5. Melanin affects the hair of both people and Himalayan rabbits.

T / F   6. The environment can affect a person's genes.

B. Work with a partner. Compare your answers in Part A. Correct the false statements.

C. Read the questions. Discuss them with the class.

1. When you want to know the main idea of a paragraph, which sentence is best to look at first?

2. What is the main idea of the whole text?
   a. The Himalayan rabbit has white fur in warm environments.
   b. The environment of a living thing is more important than its genes.
   c. Both genes and the environment affect the appearance of living things.

3. The reading talks about one part of a rabbit's environment: how warm or cold it is. What are other parts of a person's or animal's environment? Brainstorm a list of things that are part of your environment.

VOCABULARY REVIEW

Complete the sentences with the words and phrases from the box.

affect	environment	grows up	warm
are born	fur	normally	

1. When babies _____, they usually don't have much hair.

2. That animal's _____ is long and brown.

3. It's good for children to live in a safe and loving _____.

4. The weather is nice and _____. Let's go to the beach!

5. Johan's daughter wants to be a teacher when she _____.

6. I _____ go to sleep at 11 P.M.

7. Many things in our environments _____ us: the food we eat, the air we breathe, and the people we spend time with.

THINK VISUALLY

Look at the bar graph. Then discuss the questions with a partner.

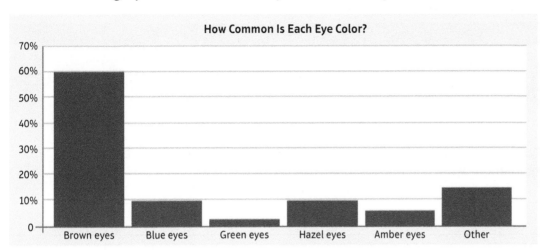

How Common Is Each Eye Color?

1. Describe the graph. What percent of people have brown, blue, green, hazel (green-brown), and amber (yellow-brown) eyes?

2. What do you think *Other* means in the graph?

3. Do most students in your class have brown eyes? Are there any students with blue, green, hazel, or amber eyes?

GRAMMAR

USING *HAVE* AND *BE* IN DESCRIPTIONS

Complete the sentences with the correct forms of *have (not)* or *be (not)*.

1. Some of the rabbits _____ black and white fur, and others are brown.

2. My parents _____ tall people. They're short.

3. Peter _____ small hands. His hands are big.

4. Dan's hair _____ curly. It's straight.

5. My cat's fur _____ black. I love black cats.

6. Aliya _____ brown eyes. They are big and pretty.

ASSIGNMENT

Write sentences to describe a close friend or family member.

PREPARE TO WRITE

A. Find a picture of the friend or family member you want to write about. Think about how to describe the person. Think about the following:

- age
- height
- eyes
- hair
- any special parts of the person's appearance

B. Work with a partner. Show your photo to your partner and describe the person. Answer your partner's questions. Then listen to your partner's description and ask questions about his or her friend or family member.

WRITE

Write a sentence to introduce your friend or family member. Then write five or more sentences about what the person looks like.

This is a photo of my (friend / brother / cousin).

_____

_____

_____

_____

_____

PROOFREAD AND EDIT

A. Proofread your sentences.

- Do you use the verbs *have* and *be* correctly?
- Are there any spelling mistakes?
- Does every sentence begin with a capital letter and end with a period?

B. Work with a partner. Share your sentences. Answer the questions in the Peer Review Form. Share your answers with your partner. Ask your partner about your sentences. Then edit them.

Peer Review Form	Yes	No
1. Does your partner write a description of the person in the picture?	☐	☐
2. Does the first sentence introduce the person?	☐	☐
3. Does your partner use adjectives correctly?	☐	☐
4. Does your partner use the verbs *have* and *be* correctly?	☐	☐
5. Are there any spelling mistakes? If there are, circle them.	☐	☐

⏵ Go to **MyEnglishLab** to complete grammar and vocabulary practices.

DEVELOP SOFT SKILLS

WORKING IN GROUPS

As a college student, you will often need to work in groups in your classes. Group work in language classes is good because it gives you more speaking practice. It is important in other classes, too. Many college professors say group work helps students learn better.

A. Read the words and definitions. You will see these words in the text.

> ### Glossary
>
> **career:** the jobs or profession that you do for a large part of your life
>
> **common:** happening often
>
> **form:** get started, begin or grow
>
> **make eye contact:** look at the eyes of someone who is looking at you
>
> **share ideas:** tell other people what you think

B. Read the text.

Group Work in Class

Getting Started

1 How do groups form in class? There are two ways:
  - Sometimes the teacher decides on the groups. He or she tells the students who to work with.
  - Sometimes the teacher says, "Find a partner" or "Work in a small group." Then the students form pairs and groups themselves.

2 Do you need a partner? Turn to a classmate. Make eye contact, smile, and ask, "Can we be partners?"

3 Do you need to join a larger group? First, find a partner. Then find more group members. Turn your chairs so that you can speak easily to the group.

4 Make sure that the people in your group know your name and that you know their names. Start by introducing yourself. It's a good idea to write down names, to help you remember them.

College students sometimes work in pairs.

Working with Your Group

5 Sometimes a teacher will give students roles (jobs to do) in their groups. These are common roles:
  - Leader: This student speaks first. He or she makes sure that all the students in the group take turns speaking.
  - Note-taker: This student takes notes.
  - Timekeeper: This student watches the clock and helps the group finish the work on time.

College students often need to work in small groups.

(Continued)

6 If you do not understand your role, ask for help. Also, make sure you understand what group's task is—what the group has to do. If you are not sure, you can say, for example, "I think we need to talk about questions 3 and 4. Is that right?"

7 When there are no special roles in your group, then everyone has the same job to do:

- think about the task
- listen to the other people in the group
- share ideas
- ask questions

8 With practice, you will get better at group-work. Learning how to work in groups is important for both your education and your career. In many jobs, people need to be good at working in pairs and on teams.

C. To work in a group in class, what do you need to do? Number the steps in order from 1 to 6.

_____ Share your ideas and listen to the other students.

__1__ Make eye contact with another student.

_____ Ask questions if you don't understand the task or your role.

_____ Turn your chairs so you can work together.

_____ Ask him or her about becoming partners.

_____ Make sure everyone in the group knows your name.

D. In Paragraph 7, you read that group work includes listening to others, sharing ideas, and asking questions. What skills do you need to do these things? Look at the list. Check (✓) the three you think are most important. Then work in a group. Compare your answers. Explain your choices. Add two more skills to the list.

☐ Speaking clearly

☐ Being a good listener

☐ Being polite

☐ Being patient

☐ Knowing how to ask questions

☐ Having a sense of humor

☐ _____

☐ _____

E. Which group work skills are you good at? Which ones do you do you need to improve? Complete the statements.

I am good at *being polite and being a good listener* .

I am good at _____

_____ .

I need to work on _____

_____ .

WHAT DID YOU LEARN?

Check (✓) the skills and vocabulary you learned. Circle the things you need to practice.

SKILLS

☐ I can identify the topic and the main idea of a text.

☐ I can describe a person's appearance.

☐ I can use *have* and *be* in descriptions.

☐ I can describe physical appearance.

☐ I can work in groups.

VOCABULARY

☐ affect   ☐ half

☐ alike   ☐ handsome

☐ appearance   ☐ mustache

☐ be born   ☐ normally

☐ beard   ☐ pair

☐ cute   ☐ pretty

☐ environment   ☐ rice

☐ fur   ☐ similar

☐ good-looking   ☐ warm

☐ grow up

⬆ Go to **MyEnglishLab** to complete a self-assessment.

Chapter 4 Sweet or Spicy?

CHAPTER PROFILE

Everyone needs food. That is a basic fact of life. But we all have different ideas about what tastes good.

This chapter is about how people feel about different foods: their food preferences. It is about how genes and the environment affect people's food preferences.

You will read about

• supertasters.

• the foods people prefer.

• the effects of your genes and your environment on your food preferences.

You will write about food preferences.

OUTCOMES

• Recognize examples

• Write about your food preferences

• Use count and noncount nouns

• Use more words for describing food

• Stay healthy

For more about **GENETICS**, see Chapter 3. See also OC **GENETICS**, Chapters 3 and 4.

GETTING STARTED

A. Look at the photos and follow the instructions.

- Put a check (✓) next to the foods that you like.
- Circle the foods that you don't know but would like to try.
- Put an X next to the foods that you don't like or that you don't want to try.

| Hamburger and French fries | Salmon sashimi | Broccoli | Chinese dumplings |

| Fruit | Korean barbecue | Blue cheese | Tacos |

B. Discuss the questions with a partner or small group.

1. Are there foods that you like? Which ones?
2. Are there foods that you want to try? Why do you want to try them?
3. Are there foods that you don't like? Which ones? Why don't you like them?

⬆ Go to **MyEnglishLab** to complete a self-assessment.

READ

SKILL: RECOGNIZING EXAMPLES

Writers give **details** to support their main ideas. There are many kinds of details. **Examples** are one kind. Writers use examples to explain their ideas. Examples help the reader understand what the writer means. Look at the paragraph below.

> Our genes affect the foods we like. Because of our genes, we like some foods, and we do not like others. For example, people with one special gene do not like bitter foods. For them, bitter foods have a very strong bad taste. These people usually prefer sweet foods, like bananas or strawberries.

Strawberries are sweet.

Kale, spinach, and broccoli are bitter.

Writers often introduce examples with **signal words**. The signal words tell the reader that an example is coming. Writers often use *for example* and *like* in this way.

- Use *for example* when the example is a full sentence:

  Our genes affect the foods we like. Because of our genes, we like some foods and we do not like others. For example, people with one special gene do not like bitter foods.

  The sentence *people with one special gene do not like bitter foods* is an example. It helps explain the idea in the first two sentences.

- Use *like* when the example is a noun or noun phrase:

  These people usually prefer sweet foods, like bananas or strawberries.

  The noun phrase *bananas or strawberries* gives details about sweet foods.

Both *for example* and *like* are signal words that help you to recognize examples. The examples give you more information about a topic. Identifying and understanding examples will help you understand key points in a text.

> **TIP**
>
> Writers sometimes give long examples to explain a difficult idea. These examples can be two or more sentences long. They can even be two or three paragraphs long. Remember that you may need to read more than one sentence to understand an example.

Complete each sentence with *like* or *for example*.

1. Carly loves meat. _____ , she eats chicken every day.

2. Bitter vegetables, _____ broccoli and spinach, are really good for your health.

3. I love chocolate things, _____ chocolate cake and chocolate ice cream.

4. Children often look like their parents. _____ , people with blue eyes often have children with blue eyes.

5. My best friend, Rodrigo, and I are very similar. _____ , we both love to try new foods, and we go to a new restaurant every weekend.

6. There are some new foods on the menu today, _____ potato dumplings and corn salad. I really want to try one of them.

> **REMEMBER**
>
> **Complete the sentences.**
>
> Writers use details, like _____ , to give more information about their main ideas. They often use _____ words to introduce examples.

VOCABULARY PREVIEW

A. Read the sentences. Look at the boldfaced words. Do you know what they mean? Share your ideas with a partner.

1. Many green vegetables are **bitter**. They are not sweet at all.

2. This soup has such a good **flavor**. I really like it.

3. **Hot** foods hurt my lips and mouth.

4. I **prefer** coffee to tea. I just like coffee more!

5. Many countries are famous for their **spicy** foods, like Mexico, India, and Thailand.

6. This coffee isn't **strong** enough. It has too much water.

7. Many fruits, like bananas and mangoes, are **sweet**.

8. The mangoes **taste** really good! Can I have some more?

She's afraid the pepper will be too hot.

Indian food is often spicy.

B. Write the boldfaced words from Part A next to their definitions.

_____ 1. like something more than other things

_____ 2. having a strong flavor because of special seeds or powders from plants

_____ 3. powerful, describing a flavor you easily notice

_____ 4. the way something tastes

_____ 5. giving a burning feeling in your mouth

_____ 6. having sugar

_____ 7. give you a flavor, like sweet or bitter, when you eat

_____ 8. having a strong, not-sweet flavor, like coffee without sugar

VOCABULARY NOTE

When we talk about food, *hot* can have two different meanings. One describes a food's temperature, like hot soup or hot coffee. The other describes foods that hurt your mouth and tongue even when they are cold, like hot peppers.

🔊 Go to **MyEnglishLab** to complete a vocabulary practice.

PREDICT

Look at the title and pictures on page 72. Check (✓) all of the information that you predict will be in the text.

☐ the meaning of *supertasters*

☐ why people like chocolate cake

☐ where to buy different types of food

☐ the part of the tongue that tastes food

READ

A. Read the text. Follow the instructions after each paragraph.

Supertasters, Genes, and the Foods We Like

1 Christy is a supertaster. What's a supertaster? It's a person who has more taste buds than most people. For a supertaster, all five flavors—sweet, bitter, sour, salty, and umami—are stronger. So Christy notices the flavors of sweet foods, like chocolate cake and ice cream, more than other people do. These foods taste *too* sweet to her. Christy is a supertaster because of her genes.

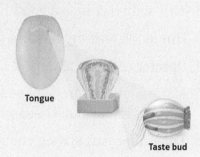

Tongue

Taste bud

1. Circle the signal word in Paragraph 1. Then underline the example. What word or phrase does the example help explain?

2 Genes affect the way foods taste to *all* of us, not just supertasters. For example, some of us have a special gene that makes us notice bitter flavors. If you have this gene, then bitter foods, like coffee or green tea, taste stronger to you than to other people. You feel the bitter flavor more than others do. People with this gene usually do not like bitter foods. Instead, they prefer sweet foods.

Chocolate cake and ice cream are sweet foods.

2. Circle the signal words in Paragraph 2. Then underline the examples. What ideas do the examples help you understand?

3 We all prefer different foods. Some of us like to eat a lot of meat, like steak or chicken. Others do not like meat at all. Some of us love hot peppers. Others do not like spicy food. What foods do you like?

The Carolina Reaper is a kind of pepper. It is the hottest pepper in the world.

3. Circle the signal word in Paragraph 3. Then underline the example. What word or phrase does the example help explain?

B. Look at your predictions again. Were they correct?

⬆ Go to **MyEnglishLab** to reread the text.

READ AGAIN

A. Read the text again. Then complete the sentences.

1. For a _____ , some foods have very strong flavors.

2. Supertasters have many _____ on their tongues.

3. The five flavors are salty, sour, umami, _____ , and _____ .

4. Some people have a special _____ that makes bitter foods taste *very* bitter.

5. Different people like different _____ .

6. Some people love _____ , like steak or chicken. Some people love hot, spicy foods, like _____ .

B. Circle the answers.

1. What's the main idea of Paragraph 1?
   a. Some foods, like ice cream and chocolate cake, are too sweet.
   b. Supertasters don't like sweet foods because of their genes.

2. What's the main idea of Paragraph 2?
   a. Genes can affect which flavors we like.
   b. Some people have a special gene for tasting bitter flavors.

3. What's the main idea of Paragraph 3?
   a. Different people like different foods.
   b. Most people like meat and spicy foods.

C. Work with a partner. Compare your answers in Parts A and B.

D. Read the questions. Discuss them with a partner.

1. Do you like sweet foods? Bitter foods? What are some examples of each kind of food?

2. Do you think you are a supertaster? Why or why not?

3. What signal words introduce examples?

VOCABULARY REVIEW

Complete the sentences with the words from the box.

bitter	flavor	hot	prefers	spicy	strong	sweet	tastes

1. Wenjing likes _____ foods, like fruit and ice cream.

2. I can't drink coffee without sugar—it's too _____ for me.

3. This chicken and rice _____ really good.

4. Sichuan food, from China, can be very _____.
   It can have a lot of peppers in it.

5. The _____ of this cake is perfect. I really like it!

6. Kenta doesn't eat much meat. He _____ fish.

Sichuan-style mapo tofu

7. The cheese has a very _____ flavor, so I only put a little on my bread.

8. The pepper is too _____! It hurts my mouth.

🔊 Go to **MyEnglishLab** to read another text.

WRITE

SKILL: WRITING ABOUT FOOD PREFERENCES

When we write about our food preferences, we write about the foods we like and the foods we do not like. We use verbs like *like*, *love*, and *hate*:

I love Italian food.

I like vegetables.

I don't like soda because I don't like sweet drinks.

I hate ice cream. It's too cold!

When we write about a general type of food, like Italian food or vegetables, we often give examples to add detail:

I like Italian food. For example, I eat pizza three times a week.

I love vegetables, like carrots and onions.

Examples give the reader more details about the foods that you like or do not like.

REMEMBER

Complete the sentences.

Use the verbs _____, _____, and
_____ to describe your food preferences.

Grammar for Writing Using count and noncount nouns

English has different types of nouns.

Most nouns are **count nouns**. They name people, places, and things we can count. They have singular and plural forms.

COUNT NOUNS

Regular		Irregular	
Singular	**Plural**	**Singular**	**Plural**
cookie	cookies	person	people
dish	dishes	man	men
tomato	tomatoes	woman	women
strawberry	strawberries	child	children

GRAMMAR NOTE

To form a plural noun:

- For most count nouns, add *s: an apple / two apples, a carrot / two carrots*
- For count nouns ending in *ch, sh, ss,* or *x,* add *es: a sandwich / two sandwiches*
- For count nouns ending in a consonant + *o,* add *es: a potato / two potatoes*
- For count nouns ending in a consonant + *y,* drop the *y* and add *ies: a cherry / two cherries*

Other nouns are **noncount nouns**. They name things we do not count. They have one form only. Do not add *s.*

NONCOUNT NOUNS

Liquids	Meats	Other Foods	Subjects and Languages	Games and Sports
water	chicken	bread	English	football
juice	fish	rice	Chinese	tennis
tea	beef	cheese	Arabic	soccer
coffee	lamb	sushi	biology	baseball

When you speak about food in general:

- use the plural form of a count noun.

    Apples are good for you.
    I like **strawberries**.

- use a singular verb with a noncount noun.

    Cheese is one of my favorite foods.
    Coffee wakes me up in the morning.

GRAMMAR NOTE

Some nouns can be both count and noncount. One example is *food*. When we speak about food in general, then we use the noncount *food*, as in *People need food to live.* When we speak about types of food, we can use the count form: *I like a lot of foods, but I don't like sweets.*

Complete the sentences.

Most nouns are _____ nouns. They can have a plural form. But _____ nouns, like the words for most liquids and types of meat, have only one form.

A. Complete the sentences with the words in parentheses. Make the count nouns plural.

Ellie enjoys most kinds of food. She loves _____ (1. egg) and _____ (2. coffee), and she has them every day for breakfast. She loves _____ (3. cheese), too—she has some every day for lunch. She also really likes _____ (4. food) from other countries, like _____ (5. sushi).

Ellie's brother, Kai, likes a lot of foods, too, especially healthy ones. He really likes fruit, like _____ (6. banana) and _____ (7. apple). He also loves _____ (8. vegetable). But Kai doesn't eat _____ (9. chicken). Kai is a vegetarian, which means he doesn't eat _____ (10. meat) or _____ (11. fish).

B. Look at the pictures. Complete the sentence for each picture. Use the correct form of the noun.

1. Carrie likes eating _____ for breakfast.

2. Carol loves to have _____ and _____ for dessert every night.

3. Shen and Benny like _____ in the morning.

4. I hate _____ for dinner because my mother makes it every night!

5. Elsa doesn't like _____. She really hates bread.

6. I love _____ ! I could eat them every day, three times a day!

C. Read the paragraph. Correct the five mistakes.

Marshall is a picky eater, which means he doesn't like a lot of foods. First and foremost, he hates vegetable. He never eats them. He also doesn't like rice, and he never eats sandwich because he doesn't like bread. But he does like breakfast foods, like egg, and he likes coffees with his breakfast. He usually has a piece of fruit with his breakfast, too. For example, he loves banana. He eats a lot of food at breakfast, but he doesn't eat much later in the day.

○ Go to **MyEnglishLab** for more grammar practice.

WRITE ABOUT YOUR FOOD PREFERENCES

STEP 1: READ TO WRITE

A. Read the words and definitions. You will see these words in the text.

> Glossary
>
> cafeteria: a place where students eat in a school or university
>
> explore: travel around a place to learn about it
>
> grad (graduate) school: a school for after students finish college, like law school or medical school
>
> miss: feel sad about (something you cannot have anymore or someone you cannot see)
>
> terrible: very bad

B. Read the emails between Sophie and Luis. Complete the sentences after each part.

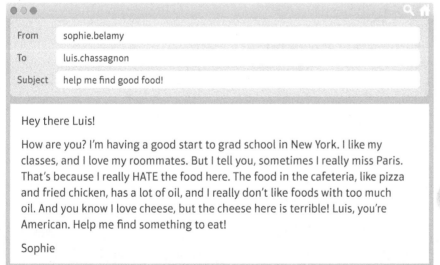

From   sophie.belamy

To   luis.chassagnon

Subject help me find good food!

Hey there Luis!

How are you? I'm having a good start to grad school in New York. I like my classes, and I love my roommates. But I tell you, sometimes I really miss Paris. That's because I really HATE the food here. The food in the cafeteria, like pizza and fried chicken, has a lot of oil, and I really don't like foods with too much oil. And you know I love cheese, but the cheese here is terrible! Luis, you're American. Help me find something to eat!

Sophie

Fried chicken

1. a. Sophie likes her _____ and her _____ in New York.

   b. She does not like _____ or the _____ in New York.

From   luis.chassagnon

To   sophie.belamy

Subject   re: help me find good food!

Hey Sophie,

Great to hear from you! Cafeteria food can be really bad, I know. But you're in New York—it has great food from all over the world. You like trying new things, so go EXPLORE the city. You like dim sum, right? So, go to Chinatown. The restaurants there are not too expensive.

I know you love Middle Eastern food, too, and there are so many places for falafel in Manhattan! I could tell you about some sushi restaurants, but the good ones are too expensive for a student, so I won't.

I know you'll find something good. In the meantime, I'll be enjoying the best foods here in Paris. :)

Good luck!

Luis

Dim sum

Falafel

2. a. Sophie likes trying _____ and eating _____ , says Luis.

    b. Sophie loves _____ , says Luis.

🔊 Go to **MyEnglishLab** to reread the text.

STEP 2: PREPARE TO WRITE

A. Circle the kinds of food that you like.

vegetables	sweet foods	Middle Eastern food
fruit	bitter foods	Indian food
meat	Chinese food	French food

B. What other kinds of food do you like? Make a list.

_____   _____

_____   _____

_____   _____

_____   _____

_____   _____

STEP 3: WRITE

Write five or more sentences about your food preferences. Include examples in at least two of your sentences. Follow the examples below.

I love eggs.

I don't like sweet fruits, like mangoes and bananas.

I really like Middle Eastern food. For example, I often get a falafel sandwich with hummus for lunch.

_____

_____

_____

_____

_____

_____

STEP 4: PROOFREAD AND EDIT

A. Proofread your sentences.

- Do you use examples to give more details about at least two of your preferences?
- Do you use *like* and *for example* correctly?
- Do you use count and noncount nouns correctly?
- Are there any spelling mistakes?

B. Work with a partner. Share your sentences. Answer the questions in the Peer Review Form. Share your answers with your partner. Ask your partner about your sentences. Then edit them.

Peer Review Form	Yes	No
1. Does your partner write about his or her preferences?	☐	☐
2. Are there at least two examples?	☐	☐
3. Does your partner use count and noncount nouns correctly?	☐	☐
4. Are there any spelling mistakes? If there are, circle them.	☐	☐

C. Read the questions. Discuss them with a partner.

1. Do you enjoy writing about your food preferences? Does it make you feel hungry? Explain.

2. Is it easy to use count and noncount nouns in your writing? Why or why not?

BUILDING VOCABULARY

USING MORE WORDS FOR DESCRIBING FOOD

There are many words related to food. In this section, you will learn words for types of food, ways of cooking, and food textures (like *soft* and *hard*).

A. Look at the photos. Put the boldfaced words into the correct columns in the chart.

Some people love **seafood**.

Dairy foods include cheese, milk, and yogurt.

Pizza can be an **oily** food.

People eat **boiled** potatoes all around the world.

Grilled chicken tastes good.

Potato chips are **crunchy**. They make a loud sound.

I eat **fried** eggs every morning.

Macaroni and cheese is a very **creamy** food.

People all over the world eat **nuts**.

These **steamed** dumplings are called *manti*.

Textures	Types of food	Ways of cooking food
oily		

B. Can you think of more words for textures, types of foods, and ways of cooking? Add them to the chart. Then compare your lists with a partner or small group.

C. Read the questions. Discuss them with a partner or in a small group.

1. Do you like seafood? What kinds of seafood do you like? How about dairy?

2. Are grilled foods healthy? Do you like grilled foods? How about steamed, fried, or boiled foods?

3. Do you like crunchy foods? How about oily or creamy foods?

◐ Go to **MyEnglishLab** to complete a vocabulary practice.

CULTURE NOTE

Vegetarians do not eat meat or fish. Some people do not eat meat, fish, or any food that comes from an animal, like milk, eggs, or honey. These people are called **vegans**. The word *vegan* can be a noun or adjective. You can say, *Jaime is a vegan* (noun) or *This soup is vegan* (adjective).

APPLY YOUR SKILLS

In this chapter, you learned about supertasters and the effect of genes on how we feel about foods. You wrote sentences about your food preferences. In Apply Your Skills, you will learn another reason we like some foods: the mere-exposure effect. You will ask other people about the foods they like and write sentences about another person's food preferences.

VOCABULARY PREVIEW

A. Read the sentences. Look at the boldfaced words and phrases. Do you know what they mean? Share your ideas with a partner.

1. Our teacher says the same things **again and again**. He always repeats himself!

2. You have only a small **amount** of food. Would you like some more?

3. Rice is a **familiar** food to billions of people all over the world.

4. We asked the professor many times to meet us in his office. **Finally**, he said yes.

5. Jermaine likes sweet foods. So he will **probably** like this cake.

6. Why did he change classes? What was the **reason** for the change?

7. Some parents give their children a **reward** for getting good grades in school.

He's measuring a small amount of sugar.

B. Write the boldfaced words and phrases from Part A next to their definitions.

_____ 1. after trying many times, or after a long wait

_____ 2. describing something that you know

_____ 3. a fact or an idea that explains why something else happens

_____ 4. many times

_____ 5. a prize or gift for doing something well

_____ 6. almost sure to be true or happen

_____ 7. how much there is of something

🔊 Go to **MyEnglishLab** to complete a vocabulary practice.

PREDICT

Look at the title and pictures on page 82. Complete the prediction about the text. Circle _a_ or _b_.

The text will be about _____ .

a. things people like and dislike

b. making foods in different countries

A. Read the text. Follow the instructions after each paragraph.

Not All Preferences Are Genetic: The Mere-Exposure Effect

1 Do you like spicy food? Can you eat hot cuisines, like Korean food, Mexican food, or Senegalese food? If you are from one of these countries, then the answer is probably *yes.* But if your country's cuisine is not very spicy, then maybe your answer is *no.* Is it because of your genes? Probably not. Scientists do not think there are genes for liking spicy foods. So what *is* the reason?

Some Mexican foods are very spicy.

> 1. Circle the signal word in Paragraph 1. Then underline the example. What word or phrase does the example help you understand?

2 One reason is the mere-exposure effect: You like people and things because they are familiar. For example, you try a new food, but you do not really like it at first. Then you eat it a second time, and a third and a fourth time. Finally, you start enjoying it. You like it because you have eaten it many times, and people prefer the foods they know well. That is the mere-exposure effect.

> 2. Circle the signal word in Paragraph 2. Then underline the example. (Hint: The example is more than one sentence.) What idea does the example help you understand?

3 Scientists believe that the mere-exposure effect can help families be healthy. We know that parents want their children to eat healthy foods, and they feed their children vegetables. But many children do not like vegetables. So parents often try to give their children rewards for eating them. For example, parents say things like, "You can eat ice cream after you eat your vegetables." But ice cream is

Many children don't like vegetables.

not healthy, and children do not usually learn to like vegetables because of a reward. So scientists tell parents to use the mere-exposure effect: Give children a small amount of a vegetable again and again. At first, they say, the children may eat very little of it. But after many meals, they will start to like it.

> 3. Circle the signal word in Paragraph 3. Then underline the example. What idea does the example help you understand?

4 Maybe the mere-exposure effect can work for you, too. For example, maybe you want to eat more vegetables. Do some vegetables, like broccoli, kale, or spinach, taste too bitter? Maybe you do not like them because of your genes. Or maybe they are just not familiar. Try eating a little bit of the vegetables every day. Then you might start to enjoy them.

4. Circle the signal words in Paragraph 4. (Hint: There are two examples in the paragraph.) Then underline the examples. What words or ideas do the examples help explain?

B. Look at your prediction again. Was it correct?

○ Go to **MyEnglishLab** to reread the text.

READ AGAIN

A. Read the text again. Then read the statements below. Circle *T* (true) or *F* (false).

T / F   1. The mere-exposure effect is about liking things because they are familiar.

T / F   2. An example of the mere-exposure effect is trying something once and liking it a lot.

T / F   3. Scientists think the mere-exposure effect can help families.

T / F   4. Rewards help children to like vegetables.

T / F   5. Scientists tell parents to give their children large amounts of vegetables at first.

T / F   6. If you want to learn to like a food, eat a little bit of it every day.

B. Match each paragraph with its main idea.

_____ 1. Paragraph 1   a. The mere-exposure effect is one reason that people like things.

_____ 2. Paragraph 2   b. You can use the mere-exposure effect to learn to like different foods.

_____ 3. Paragraph 3   c. Why do some people like spicy food, but others don't?

_____ 4. Paragraph 4   d. Parents can get their children to eat healthy foods with the mere-exposure effect.

C. Work with a partner. Compare your answers in Parts A and B. Correct the false statements in Part A.

D. Read the questions. Discuss them with a partner or in a small group.

1. Do you ever think about changing your eating habits (the foods that you often eat)? Explain.

2. Do you think the mere-exposure effect can work for adults? Why or why not?

VOCABULARY REVIEW

Complete the sentences with the words and phrases from the box.

again and again	familiar	probably	rewards
amount	finally	reason	

1. I don't feel well. I _____ won't go out to eat with you tonight.

2. If you don't like a food, try eating it _____. Then maybe you'll like it.

3. Children like to get _____ for doing something that their parents want.

4. There is a small _____ of sugar in the coffee. It tastes a little sweet.

5. Some people don't like bitter foods. Their genes are often the _____ for this feeling.

6. After trying sushi many times, Sami _____ started to enjoy it.

7. The shop had 30 kinds of ice cream. Some were _____ flavors, like chocolate and coffee, but others were new to me.

THINK VISUALLY

Look at the graph. It shows the results of a survey of students at a university in the United States. Then answer the questions.

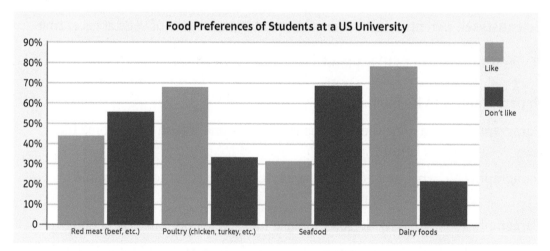

1. With a partner, describe the graph. What foods do students at the university like most? What do they like least? Does anything surprise you?

2. Think about students from your country. How are their food preferences the same as those of students in the survey? How are they different? Explain.

GRAMMAR

USING COUNT AND NONCOUNT NOUNS

Circle the correct words to complete the sentences.

1. Hari loves **chicken / chickens**. He eats it for lunch every day.

2. My parents really like **vegetable / vegetables**, like broccoli and kale.

3. Kara and Steve don't like **coffee / coffees**. It's too bitter for them.

4. I'm going to the store because I need **egg / eggs** for breakfast tomorrow.

5. I'd like a small piece of fried **fish / fishes**.

6. Jin Young always drinks **water / waters** after she exercises.

ASSIGNMENT

Interview three classmates. Then write about one person's food preferences.

PREPARE TO WRITE

A. You will interview three students about the foods that they like. First, write at least five foods in the first column of the chart. You can write specific foods (like *carrots* or *falafel*) or types of food (like *vegetables* or *Middle Eastern food)*.

Foods	Name of Student 1 _____	Name of Student 2 _____	Name of Student 3 _____

B. Ask three classmates if they like the foods in your list. Fill in the chart with their names and answers. Ask for examples of types of foods.

> A: Do you like vegetables?
>
> B: Yes, I do.
>
> A: Can you give me some examples?
>
> B: I like kale and corn.

WRITE

Choose one of the students you interviewed. Write sentences about five or more of his or her food preferences. Include examples.

_____

_____

_____

_____

_____

_____

_____

PROOFREAD AND EDIT

A. Proofread your sentences.

- Do you use the verbs _like, love,_ and _hate_ correctly?

- Do you use the signal words _like_ and _for example_ correctly?

- Are there any spelling mistakes?

B. Work with the student whose food preferences you wrote about. Share your sentences. Answer the questions in the Peer Review Form. Share your answers with your partner. Ask your partner about your sentences. Then edit them.

Peer Review Form	Yes	No
1. Does your partner write about your food preferences?	☐	☐
2. Is the information about your preferences correct?	☐	☐
3. Does your partner use the verbs _like, love,_ and _hate_ correctly?	☐	☐
4. Does your partner use the signal words _for example_ and _like_ correctly?	☐	☐
5. Are there any spelling mistakes? If there are, circle them.	☐	☐

◐ Go to **MyEnglishLab** to complete grammar and vocabulary practices.

DEVELOP SOFT SKILLS

STAYING HEALTHY

If you are like most college students, you are very busy with things like going to class, studying, and being with friends. That leaves no time for being sick! Being sick can mean not feeling well enough to do school work or even missing class. So how can you stay healthy? Getting enough sleep and eating well are two keys to healthy living.

A. Read the words and definitions. You will see these words in the text.

Glossary

junk food: food that is not good for you because it has too much sugar or fat

kept getting sick: continued to become sick again and again

skip: not do (something you usually do or should do)

snack: something small you eat when it's not time for breakfast, lunch, or dinner

take care of yourself: make sure you have the things you need to be happy and healthy

waste: use (money, time, skills) in a way that does no good

B. Read the text. Rose is a senior in college. She is writing her brother Peter, who is in his first year at a different university.

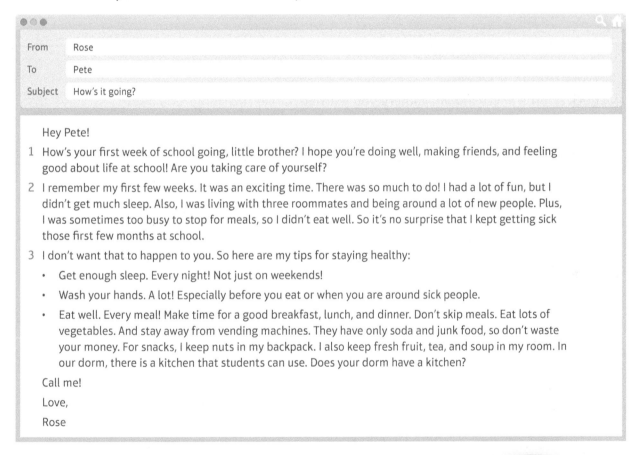

From   Rose

To   Pete

Subject   How's it going?

Hey Pete!

1 How's your first week of school going, little brother? I hope you're doing well, making friends, and feeling good about life at school! Are you taking care of yourself?

2 I remember my first few weeks. It was an exciting time. There was so much to do! I had a lot of fun, but I didn't get much sleep. Also, I was living with three roommates and being around a lot of new people. Plus, I was sometimes too busy to stop for meals, so I didn't eat well. So it's no surprise that I kept getting sick those first few months at school.

3 I don't want that to happen to you. So here are my tips for staying healthy:

- Get enough sleep. Every night! Not just on weekends!
- Wash your hands. A lot! Especially before you eat or when you are around sick people.
- Eat well. Every meal! Make time for a good breakfast, lunch, and dinner. Don't skip meals. Eat lots of vegetables. And stay away from vending machines. They have only soda and junk food, so don't waste your money. For snacks, I keep nuts in my backpack. I also keep fresh fruit, tea, and soup in my room. In our dorm, there is a kitchen that students can use. Does your dorm have a kitchen?

Call me!

Love,

Rose

C. What tips does Rose give Peter? Check (✓) all the topics she gives her brother tips about.

☐ making friends   ☐ skipping meals

☐ sleeping   ☐ spending money on snacks

☐ studying   ☐ eating healthy snacks

☐ washing hands   ☐ cooking

D. What do you think about Rose's tips? Complete the sentences in the chart. Share your ideas with a partner. How are your ideas similar? How are they different?

Tips from Rose	Rose's Tips That I Follow	Rose's Tips That Are Hard for Me to Follow
It's a good idea to ___ ___ ___ .	I (always / usually) ___ ___ ___ .	I should ___ ___ but that's hard because ___ ___ .

E. In a small group, write two more tips for college students on how to stay healthy.

1. _____

2. _____

WHAT DID YOU LEARN?

Check (✓) the skills and vocabulary you learned. Circle the things you need to practice.

SKILLS

☐ I can recognize examples.   ☐ I can use words for describing food.

☐ I can write about food preferences.   ☐ I can stay healthy.

☐ I can use count and noncount nouns.

VOCABULARY

☐ again and again   ☐ flavor   ☐ reward

☐ amount   ☐ fried   ☐ seafood

☐ bitter   ☐ grilled   ☐ spicy

☐ boiled   ☐ hot   ☐ steamed

☐ creamy   ☐ nut   ☐ strong

☐ crunchy   ☐ oily   ☐ sweet

☐ dairy foods   ☐ prefer   ☐ taste

☐ familiar   ☐ probably

☐ finally   ☐ reason

⊙ Go to **MyEnglishLab** to complete a self-assessment.

⊙ Go to **MyEnglishLab** for a challenge reading about Genetics.

Business and Technology

Go to **MyEnglishLab** to to see an introduction about **BUSINESS AND TECHNOLOGY.**

Chapter 5 | Mobile-First Design

CHAPTER PROFILE

Business is about the companies that sell products and provide services. **Technology** refers to new machines and other equipment and to new ways of doing things that use computers or are based on a modern understanding of science.

This chapter is about how companies design apps and websites to advertise and sell their products and services.

You will read about

• mobile-first design.

• people's opinions of mobile apps.

• the designs of two mobile websites.

You will write about smartphones, computers, and apps.

For more about **BUSINESS AND TECHNOLOGY**, see Chapter 6. See also [OC] **BUSINESS AND TECHNOLOGY**, Chapters 5 and 6.

OUTCOMES

• Recognize connections between ideas

• Use *but, and, also,* and *too* in sentences

• Use *can* for ability and possibility

• Use vocabulary for smartphone users

• Communicate with instructors

GETTING STARTED

Look at the photo at the bottom of the page and answer the questions.

1. What are the people doing?

2. Look at the types of smartphone apps in the list. (Apps are programs that you can download to your phone.) Check (✓) the ones that you like to use.

   ☐ social media apps (like Facebook™, Twitter™, WeChat™, WhatsApp™)

   ☐ photo and video sharing apps (like Instagram™, YouTube™, Snapchat™)

   ☐ shopping apps

   ☐ food service apps

   ☐ gaming apps

   ☐ learning apps

   ☐ health apps

3. Share your answers to Questions 1 and 2 with a partner or in a small group. What are examples of the types of apps that you like? Why do you like them?

VOCABULARY NOTE

Use the verb **download** when you talk about moving programs or other files from the Internet to your phone or a computer: *I **downloaded** this app for free.* Use **upload** or **post** when you talk about putting pictures or videos on a website for other people to see: *It's taking a long time to **upload** this video. I **post** pictures on social media almost every day.*

🔊 Go to **MyEnglishLab** to complete a self-assessment.

READ

SKILL: RECOGNIZING CONNECTIONS BETWEEN IDEAS

When you read, it is important to see **connections** between ideas in the text. Sometimes one word will make a connection clear to you. For example, the word *because* does this.

> Most companies now have websites because ...

You can predict what will come next: The second part of the sentence will explain *why* most companies now have websites.

> Most companies now have websites **because** so many people go online to learn about products and services.

The words *but* and *and* also show connections between ideas in a text.

But

But signals a **contrast**. Sentences with *but* tell how two people, things, situations, or ideas are different from each other.

> Desktop computers are big, **but** smartphones are small.

> I have a smartphone, **but** I don't have a desktop computer.

When you see *but* in a sentence, you can predict that contrasting information is coming.

A laptop is larger than a smartphone **but** smaller than a desktop computer.

And

And is used to **add information**. After *and,* you can predict there will be more of the same kind of information.

> My smartphone is fun **and** easy to use.

> On a smartphone, you can shop online **and** check email.

The words *too* and *also* show the same kind of connection as *and*.

> My smartphone is fun. It's easy to use, **too**.

> My smartphone is fun. It's **also** easy to use.

And, too, and *also* can be used to show how things are similar.

> Both my smartphone **and** my laptop are small **and** light. They are **also** very useful.
> I bring my smartphone with me everywhere I go, **and** I often bring my laptop, **too**.

REMEMBER

Complete the sentences.

1. The word _____ introduces a contrast or difference.

2. The words _____ , _____ , and _____ can be used to show how things are similar.

VOCABULARY PREVIEW

A. Read the sentences. Look at the boldfaced words and phrases. Do you know what they mean? Share your ideas with a partner.

1. Use your computer to **access** the Internet anywhere on campus.

2. In 2000, there were about six billion (6,000,000,000) people in the world. By 2050, there may be **billions** more.

3. Companies **design** their websites to look good and be easy to use.

4. The classroom is small. Only about 20 desks can **fit** inside.

5. I need to **focus on** my work right now. I have no time to think about anything else.

6. Jared has a new phone, and the **screen** is really big.

7. The metal ball on the left has a plain and **simple** design, but the design of the metal object on the right is complicated.

8. This app is so **useful**! It helps you to save money.

> **VOCABULARY NOTE**
>
> *Design* can be a noun or a verb. Here it is a noun: *I love the **design** of this new phone.* Here it is a verb: *Architects **design** buildings.*

B. Write the boldfaced words and phrases from Part A next to their definitions.

_____ 1. the part of a phone, computer, or TV where you see words and pictures

_____ 2. be able to enter and use something

_____ 3. give all your attention to something

_____ 4. describing a style or design that is plain, not complicated

_____ 5. make something for a specific use or to look a certain way

_____ 6. describing something that helps you to do what you want to do

_____ 7. a large number, more than 1,000,000,000

_____ 8. have enough space to go into or be in (a place)

⬆ Go to **MyEnglishLab** to complete a vocabulary practice.

Read the title of the text. What do you think it means? Write your idea and share it with a partner.

_____

_____

_____

READ

> **VOCABULARY NOTE**
>
> **Mobile websites** are sites that are made for a smartphone's Internet **browser**. (Examples of browsers are Safari®, Firefox™, and Chrome™.)
>
> **Apps**, or applications, on your phone also let you access information on the Internet. Apps are usually easier to use than mobile websites.

A. Read the text and answer the question after each paragraph.

Start Small, Then Build Bigger: Mobile-First Design

1 Are you one of the billions of people around the world who use smartphones? Is your smartphone the main way you access the Internet? Just a few years ago, people used big desktop computers to shop online, check email, or watch videos. But now, you can use your smartphone to do all those things, and much more.

> 1. Circle *but* in Paragraph 1. What does it contrast?
>   a. shopping online and checking email
>   b. what people did in the past and what they can do now
>   c. people who have smartphones and people who don't

2 The way people use smartphones is changing the way companies design their websites. In the past, companies designed websites for big desktop screens. They put a lot of information on a company's homepage because you could see a lot on the big screen. But all that information does not fit on a small screen. So today, companies focus on designing simple websites for smartphones. They put only the most useful and important information on their mobile websites. After they make a good site for a smartphone, they make one for a bigger screen. This process (the way to make something) is called *mobile-first design*.

> 2. Circle *but* in Paragraph 2. What does it contrast?
>   a. apps and websites
>   b. homepages and other web pages
>   c. the amount of information that fits on big and small screens

3 Look at the two examples below. Web page A shows an e-commerce site (a website that sells a lot of things, like Amazon®, Alibaba™, or Souq.com™) on a smartphone. There are just a few words. There are also just a few pictures. The design for the site is simple, and the site looks easy to use. Web page B shows the website for the same company but on a desktop computer. It has more words and more pictures, but it looks easy to use, too.

3. Paragraph 3 compares two web pages. How are they similar, and how are they different? Circle your answers.

a. the reasons why people use these web pages   similar / different

b. the kind of screen where you see each web page   similar / different

c. the number of words and photos on each web page   similar / different

d. how easy it looks to use each web page   similar / different

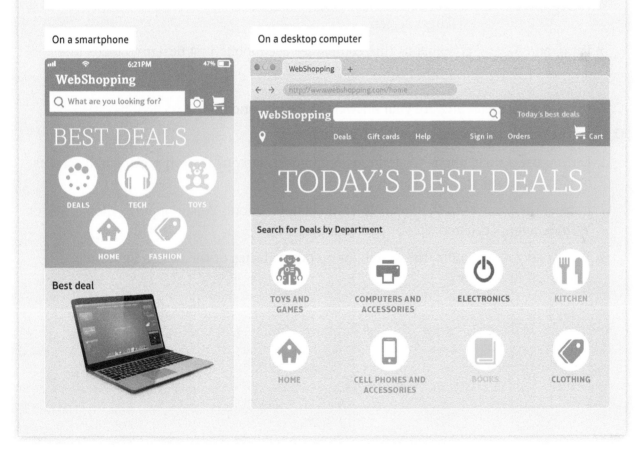

On a smartphone   On a desktop computer

B. Look at your prediction about the title again. Was it correct?

⏺ Go to **MyEnglishLab** to reread the text.

READ AGAIN

A. Read the text again. Then complete the sentences with the words from the box.

billions	information	mobile	mobile-first design	screens	shop online

Today, (1) _____ of people use smartphones all over the world. They use their phones to do things like check their email and (2) _____ . Because of smartphones, companies design their websites for small (3) _____ first. There usually aren't a lot of words on (4) _____ websites. These sites have only the most important and useful (5) _____ . Later, companies make their websites for bigger screens. This way of doing things is called (6) _____ : designing for small screens first and then designing for bigger ones.

B. Draw a line to connect each paragraph with its main idea.

1. Paragraph 1…   a. tells the reader that billions of people are using smartphones now.

2. Paragraph 2…   b. compares a web page on a smartphone with a web page on a larger screen.

3. Paragraph 3…   c. explains that companies use mobile-first design to focus first on smartphones.

C. Work with a partner. Compare your answers in Parts A and B.

D. Read the questions. Discuss them with a partner.

1. Do you use a smartphone? A desktop computer? A laptop? Do you prefer small screens or larger screens?

2. Look at the pictures in the text. Which do you like more, WebShopping's mobile site or WebShopping's desktop site? Explain your answer.

3. Which do you like more, the design for mobile websites or the design for desktops? Explain your answer.

VOCABULARY REVIEW

Complete the sentences with the words from the box.

access	design	focus on	simple
billions	fit	screen	useful

1. Only a few pictures can _____ on the homepage of a mobile website.

2. This app is really _____. It helps me to eat less!

3. You can _____ the Internet anywhere in the building through WiFi.

4. The _____ on my laptop is small. I prefer to watch shows on my TV.

5. _____ of people use the Internet every day.

6. The company's homepage is very _____. There are only a few words and photos on it.

7. Companies spend a lot of time and money to _____ websites that are easy to use.

8. Stop playing on your phone! We have to _____ our project so we can finish it on time.

◑ Go to **MyEnglishLab** to read another text.

WRITE

SKILL: USING *BUT, AND, ALSO,* AND *TOO* IN SENTENCES

And and *But*

And and *but* have different meanings, but they are used in the same way in sentences. They can connect two words, two phrases, or two sentences. When you connect two sentences, use a comma before *and* or *but*.

Connecting two words	My smartphone is *small* **and** *light*.
	Smartphones are *small* **but** *expensive*.
Connecting two phrases	My smartphone is *easy to use* **and** *fun to play with*.
	I take my smartphone *everywhere I go*—**but** *not in the shower!*
Connecting two sentences	*My smartphone is old,* **and** *I want a new one.*
	My smartphone is old, **but** *I am happy with it.*

Too and *Also*

Too and *also* are similar in meaning, but they are not used the same way in sentences.

- Put *too* at the end of a sentence. Use a comma before *too*.

  I check email on my laptop. I check it on my phone, too.

  My smartphone is easy to use. It's fun to play with, too.

- *Also* usually goes before the main verb in a sentence.

  I want a new phone. I **also want** a new laptop.

  I can shop on my phone. I **can also play** games on it.

- Put *also* after the verb when the main verb is *be*.

  Smartphones are easy to use. They **are also** fun to play with.

  My laptop is old. It's **also** heavy.

GRAMMAR NOTE

Do not use *also* or *too* in sentences with negative verbs. Use *either*: I **don't have** a desktop computer, and I **don't have** a laptop, **either.**

Use *and*, *also*, *too*, or *but* to complete the sentences.

1. I have a desktop computer. I _____ have a laptop.

2. This website is easy to use, _____ that site is not.

3. You can use Instagram to share pictures _____ send messages.

4. The company sells clothes _____ sports equipment.

5. My phone is old _____ still good.

6. WebShopping is my favorite app. Maria really likes it, _____ .

7. This game is very popular. It's _____ free to download.

REMEMBER

Complete the sentences.

1. You can put two sentences together with _____ or _____ . Use a comma.

2. Put _____ at the end of a sentence. Use a comma.

3. Put _____ before the main verb in most sentences, but put it after the verb *be*.

Grammar for Writing Using *can* for ability and possibility

We use **can** with the base form of a verb to describe abilities and possibilities (things that may happen). The negative forms of *can* are *cannot* and *can't*.

CAN			
Subject	*Can (+ not)*	**Base Form of Verb**	
Alan You	**can**	speak take	English. good pictures on this phone.
I You	**cannot** **can't**	sing find	well. hotel rooms with this app.

REMEMBER

Complete the sentences.

1. Use *can* to talk about abilities and _____.

2. Use the negative form _____ or _____ when something is not possible, or when someone is unable to do something or does not know how to do it.

A. Use *can* or *can't* with the verbs shown to complete the sentences.

I love my new tablet. It's really light, so I _____ (1. bring) it with me wherever I go. Its battery is excellent, too. I _____ (2. work) on it for ten hours without needing to charge it. The camera isn't great, so I _____ (3. take) good pictures. But I don't take many pictures anyway.

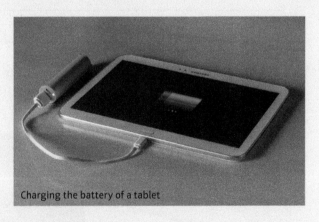

Charging the battery of a tablet

Most importantly, I _____ (4. use) it for my clothing business. I _____ (5. go) to flea markets with my tablet and sell my clothes directly to customers. My customers _____ (6. use) their credit cards, and they _____ (7. look at) their sales information on the big screen of my tablet. My smartphone screen is too small, so customers _____ (8. see) information on the screen easily. My tablet is much better!

CULTURE NOTE

Flea markets are places to buy new and used clothes, antiques (old and often valuable furniture, jewelry, and other items), plants, food, and other goods. The goods are often made locally (near the market). Flea markets are usually outdoors.

B. Look at the list below. Can you do these things with your phone? Check (✓) the boxes next to what you *can* do. Put an ✗ in the boxes next to what you *can't* do. Discuss your answers with a partner.

☐ call friends and family on my phone   ☐ find a good restaurant with my phone

☐ watch movies on my phone   ☐ control my car with my phone

☐ take pictures with my phone   ☐ check email on my phone

☐ read books on my phone   ☐ swim with my phone

☐ listen to music on my phone   ☐ turn on the TV with my phone

C. Using the list above, write at least six sentences about things you *can* and *can't* do with your phone.

I can call friends and family on my phone.

_____

_____

_____

_____

_____

_____

_____

● Go to **MyEnglishLab** for more grammar practice.

WRITE ABOUT SIMILARITIES AND DIFFERENCES
STEP 1: READ TO WRITE

A. Read the words and definitions. You will see these words in the text.

Glossary

account: an arrangement with a company that allows you to use their services

compare: look at two or more things to see if they are similar or different

push notification: a message on the lock screen of a mobile phone or tablet

sneakers: shoes for walking, running, or playing sports

well-designed: describing something that was carefully planned and made

---

There are three push notifications on this screen.

B. Read what people think about WebShopping's mobile app. Circle the correct word(s) to complete the sentence after each review.

Babi G.

São Paolo, Brazil

★ ★ ★ ★ ★

I love shopping, and I love the new WebShopping app! It's well-designed and easy to use. The browser-based site for my laptop is well-designed, too, and it's also easy to use, but the smartphone app is better. It sends me push notifications when things are on sale. The browser-based site doesn't do that.

Now that WebShopping has a mobile app, I can shop wherever I go!

---

1. The reviewer **likes / doesn't like** the WebShopping app.

Taka S.
Osaka, Japan
★★★★★

This app isn't that good. The main reason is this: If you don't have a WebShopping account, you always get log-in screens that ask you to sign up for an account, like this ➜

You can't use the app easily without an account—I hate that! Their browser-based site on my laptop is better. There aren't any sign-up screens there.

Not a fan of the mobile app at all.

2. The reviewer **likes / doesn't like** the WebShopping app.

Kai E.
Los Angeles, United States
★★★★★

This new app is ok, but I still prefer to shop on my laptop. A lot more fits on the bigger screen. For example, when you look at sneakers, you can put two, three, or four different styles on the screen at the same time. But you can't do this with the app—you can look at only one pair at a time. Sure, you can find anything you want on the app, but you can't compare things easily.

3. The reviewer prefers the WebShopping **app / browser-based site on his laptop.**

C. Work with a partner. Complete the Venn diagram with the following information from the reviews.

TIP

Use a Venn diagram with two circles when you want to compare two things. In the middle (the part shared by both circles), write facts that are true for both things. In the other two areas, write facts that are true for only one thing or the other.

good design
easy to use
sends push notifications
no push notifications
you can shop wherever you go
too many sign-up screens
no sign-up screens
you can look at many things at the same time
you can't compare things easily
you can find anything you want

WebShopping's mobile app

Both

WebShopping's browser-based site for a computer

• sends push notifications

• good design

D. Use the information from Part C to write three sentences about WebShopping's app and its browser-based website for a computer. Use *and*, *also*, *too*, or *but* in each sentence.

1. _The WebShopping app sends push notifications, but the browser-based site doesn't have any._

2. _____

3. _____

4. _____

🔊 Go to **MyEnglishLab** to reread the text.

STEP 2: PREPARE TO WRITE

A. Read the questions. Discuss them with a partner.

1. Where do you use your smartphone? Where do you use your laptop, desktop, or tablet?

2. How often do you use your phone? How often do you use your laptop, desktop, or tablet?

3. What do you use your phone for? What do you use your laptop, desktop, or tablet for?

4. Are there things that you can do *only* with your phone? Are there things that you can do *only* on your laptop, desktop, or tablet? Explain.

B. Complete the Venn diagram with the ideas from your discussion in Part A.

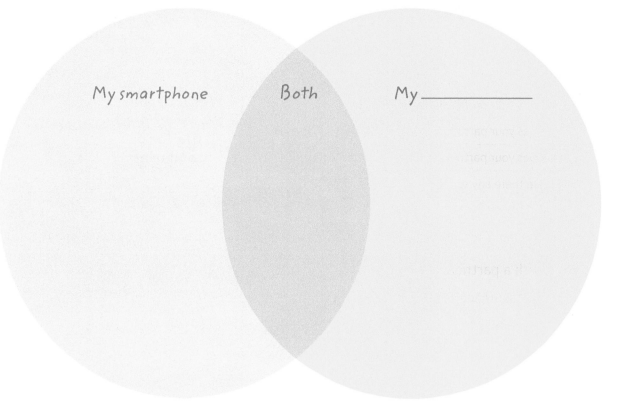

My smartphone   Both   My _____

STEP 3: WRITE

Write five or more sentences that describe the similarities and differences between your smartphone and a desktop or laptop. In two or more sentences, use *can* or *can't*. In two or more sentences, use *and, also, too,* or *but*.

_____

_____

_____

_____

_____

_____

STEP 4: PROOFREAD AND EDIT

A. Proofread your sentences.

- Do you use *and*, *also*, *too*, and *but* correctly?

- Do you use commas correctly?

- Do you use *can* and *can't* correctly?

- Are there any spelling mistakes?

B. Work with a partner. Share your sentences. Answer the questions in the Peer Review Form. Share your answers with your partner. Ask your partner about your sentences. Then edit them.

Peer Review Form	Yes	No
1. Does your partner write about similarities and differences between his or her smartphone and a laptop, desktop, or tablet?	☐	☐
2. Does your partner use *and*, *also*, *too*, and *but* correctly?	☐	☐
3. Does your partner use commas correctly?	☐	☐
4. Does your partner use *can* or *can't* correctly?	☐	☐
5. Are there any spelling mistakes? If there are, circle them.	☐	☐

C. Work with a partner. Answer the questions.

1. Which sentence is true for you? Check (✔) and circle your answer. Then explain.

   ☐ I use my phone and my **laptop / desktop / tablet** to do the same things.

   ☐ I use my phone and my **laptop / desktop / tablet** in very different ways.

2. Can you use *and*, *also*, *too*, and *but* to connect ideas? Which words are easy to use? Which words are difficult? Explain.

BUILDING VOCABULARY

USING VOCABULARY FOR SMARTPHONE USERS

Here are some more words that we use when talking about our smartphones and how we use them.

A. Read the sentences. Then look at the pictures and write the correct boldfaced words below them.

a. You don't always need words. You can send **emojis** instead. They're fun!

b. Aisha is going to **stream** a video for her online class.

c. **Tap** the screen of your smartphone to open the app that you want to use.

d. Clara uses **earbuds** to listen to music. They are nice and small.

e. The **icons** for all my apps can't fit on one screen.

f. Michael is sliding a finger up the screen of his tablet to **scroll** down and keep reading.

g. Do you **text** your friends?

1. _____ 2. _____ 3. _____

4. _____ 5. _____

6. _____ 7. _____

B. Look at how the boldfaced words in Part A are used in the sentences. Write them in the chart.

Nouns	Verbs
emojis	stream

C. Match the items with the ways to use them.

_____ 1. earbuds

_____ 2. emojis

_____ 3. icons

_____ 4. web pages

a. **Text** these to friends to show your feelings.

b. Use these to listen to music or videos that you **stream**.

c. **Scroll** through these to find information.

d. **Tap** on these to open apps.

D. Read the questions. Discuss them with a partner or in a small group.

1. Do you text a lot? Who do you text most often? What are your favorite emojis?

2. Do you stream music or movies or other videos? What sites or apps do you use?

3. What apps or sites do you use to find restaurants to go to or other things to do in your local area? Explain your answers.

⊙ Go to **MyEnglishLab** to complete a vocabulary practice.

APPLY YOUR SKILLS

In this chapter, you learned about mobile-first design and you read reviews of a mobile app. You wrote sentences about the similarities and differences between a smartphone and a desktop, laptop, or tablet. In Apply Your Skills, you will learn more about the design of mobile apps. You will then write about the similarities and differences between two apps.

VOCABULARY PREVIEW

A. Read the sentences. Look at the boldfaced words. Do you know what they mean? Share your ideas with a partner.

1. You can do many **activities** at my school's sports center: You can get some exercise, or you can watch people play sports.

2. I hate that there are so many clothing and gaming **ads** in this app.

3. Academic advisors **guide** college students through the process of choosing courses.

4. There are three color **options** for this phone: black, white, and red.

5. There are always lots of **reviews** on sites for local restaurants.

6. Classroom **rule** #1: Do not text anyone during class.

7. This app is **useless**. It doesn't help me to do anything.

8. There are billions of social media **users** across the world.

B. Write the boldfaced words from Part A next to their definitions.

_____ 1. show someone the right way to do something

_____ 2. something that tells people what they must do

_____ 3. people who use something, usually a product or service

_____ 4. opinions on products or services that people write on websites

_____ 5. things to do

_____ 6. things that are possible, that you can choose among

_____ 7. not useful

_____ 8. pictures or words that companies use to get you to buy things, short for *advertisements*

DISCOUNT UP TO
BEST **50**% **SALE**
BIG OFFER

An ad for a sale

🔊 Go to **MyEnglishLab** to complete a vocabulary practice.

PREDICT

Look at the title of the blog. Then look at the pictures. Which do you think is the better mobile site, Backpack or TravelGuide? _____

VOCABULARY NOTE

A **blog** is a website where one person posts information or opinions, usually on one subject.

READ

A. Read the text. Complete the sentence after each paragraph.

Tim's Travel Blog, Post #16

Backpack or TravelGuide: Which is the better mobile site?

1 Everyone talks about the best travel sites. And we always hear the same two names: Backpack and TravelGuide. They both have lots of information on hotels, restaurants, and activities. They both have lots of user reviews, too. But which site is better? The answer is easy: Backpack. Let me explain.

---

1. The writer wants to compare _____.

   a. two travel sites

   b. restaurants, hotels, and activities

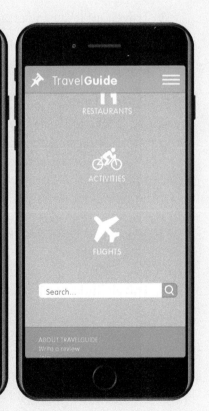

2 It is all about the homepage. On Backpack, the first thing you see is a question, *What are you looking for?* Under that, there are three icons, for hotels, restaurants, and things to do. The question guides you to choose one of the three options. All of this fits "above the fold." That means it is on the part of the page that you can see without scrolling down. So on Backpack, you can easily find and choose what you want.

2. You can _____ on the homepage.

   a. answer three questions

   b. find and choose things easily

3 On TravelGuide, the first thing you see is a big photo. You cannot tap on it—it is just something to look at. Below the photo, there is a hotels icon, but it is all the way down near the bottom of the screen. Below that icon, you see half of another icon. What is it? A restaurant icon? An advertisement? Nobody knows! You must scroll down to see more. That's where you finally find most of the important information: the restaurants icon, the activities icon, the flights icon, and a search bar.

3. TravelGuide has a restaurants icon, but _____ .

   a. you cannot tap on it

   b. it is not easy to see on the homepage

4 In short, Backpack's design is better than TravelGuide's. Backpack has three useful and important icons on its homepage, and you do not need to scroll down to find them. You can easily see everything you need. But TravelGuide shows a useless photo first and then only one and a half icons. You cannot see the whole homepage without scrolling. Only Backpack follows two important rules in mobile-first design: (1) show only the most important information, and (2) make the site easy for users. So Backpack is definitely the better mobile site.

4. TravelGuide has a photo on its homepage that _____ .

   a. helps you use the site

   b. gives no important information

B. Look at your prediction again. Was it correct?

⊙ Go to **MyEnglishLab** to reread the text.

READ AGAIN

A. Read the text again. Then write the paragraph number next to its main idea.

_____ 1. The homepage for TravelGuide is not very good.

_____ 2. Backpack has lots of useful information on its homepage.

_____ 3. Backpack is better because it follows two important mobile-first rules.

_____ 4. There are two popular mobile travel sites, but one is better.

B. Work with a partner. Complete the Venn diagram with the notes below.

a question on the homepage	many user reviews
a large photo on the homepage	only one and a half icons above the fold on the homepage
all important icons above the fold on the homepage	a hotels icon on the homepage
a flights icon on the homepage	information on many things, like hotels, restaurants, and activities
user must scroll down to find the most important information	

Backpack   Both   TravelGuide

C. Look at the information in the Venn diagram on page 111. Complete the sentences with *and*, *also*, *too*, or *but*. Add commas where they are needed.

1. The Backpack mobile site has many user reviews. There are _____ many user reviews on TravelGuide.

2. The TravelGuide mobile site has information on restaurants and activities. Backpack has a lot of information on these things _____ .

3. Backpack has a question on its homepage _____ TravelGuide doesn't. It has a large photo.

4. There's a hotels icon on the homepages of both TravelGuide _____ Backpack.

5. TravelGuide has a flights icon _____ Backpack doesn't have one.

6. You must scroll down to find useful information on TravelGuide _____ you can find the information without scrolling on Backpack.

7. Backpack shows you the most important information on its homepage _____ it makes the site easy for you to use.

D. Read the questions. Discuss them with a partner or in a small group.

1. Think of two or more sites that you use for travel information or information about local businesses. Which site do you like better? Why?

2. Think of an app or a mobile site. Then look at the company's site on a desktop or laptop. What are the similarities and differences between the two? Which do you like better?

VOCABULARY REVIEW

Complete the sentences with the words from the box.

activities	guide	reviews	useless
ads	options	rule	users

1. If you don't know where you are going, use this maps app. It will _____ you to the restaurant.

2. Where would you like to have dinner? There are several good _____ in this neighborhood.

3. Only people with accounts can post _____ .

4. Millions of _____ visit the site every day.

5. Social media apps often have a lot of _____ . Usually they are for products and services that you like.

6. The only _____ in class is no eating. Food can make the classroom smell bad.

7. There are so many different _____ for us in New York. There's a lot we can do!

8. My car is _____ ! It's very old, and I can't drive it anymore.

THINK VISUALLY

Look at the two pie charts (also called *circle graphs*). They show the results from a recent survey question about Americans' smartphone use: *What do you do most on your phone?* The top answers are in the graphs.

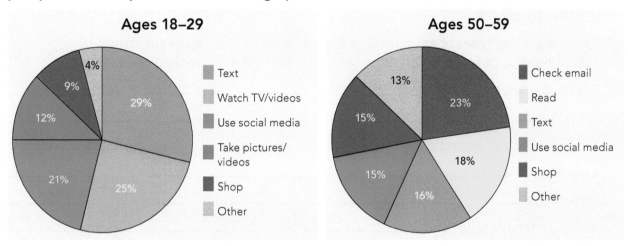

Ages 18–29

- 29% Text
- 25%
- 21%
- 12%
- 9%
- 4%

- Text
- Watch TV/videos
- Use social media
- Take pictures/videos
- Shop
- Other

Ages 50–59

- 23% Check email
- 18%
- 16%
- 15%
- 15%
- 13%

- Check email
- Read
- Text
- Use social media
- Shop
- Other

1. Look at the graphs. Compare the ways that 18- to 29-year-olds and 50- to 65-year-olds use their phones. What's similar? What's different?

2. Are you surprised by the survey results? Do you think people in your country use their phones like people in the United States? Explain.

GRAMMAR

USING *CAN* FOR ABILITY AND POSSIBILITY

Complete the sentences with *can* or *can't* + the verb in parentheses.

1. You _____ (find) helpful user reviews on some sites.

2. I _____ (use) my phone. The battery died, so I need to charge it.

3. This app is great! You _____ (stream) videos for free on it.

4. Mike doesn't know the address. Call or text Lea. She _____ (give) it to you.

5. Brittany doesn't have her phone. So she _____ (send) you any photos of the party right now.

6. I _____ (see) the text or pictures on this site. They're too small. The site isn't designed well.

ASSIGNMENT

Write sentences about the similarities and differences between two apps.

PREPARE TO WRITE

A. There are many types of apps. Look at the categories below. Write the names of two or more apps for each category. Some apps can go in more than one category.

Messaging apps: _____

Social media apps: _____

Photo and video sharing apps: _____

Local-search apps: _____

News apps: _____

Music streaming apps: _____

Map apps: _____

B. Choose two apps to write about from one of the categories. Use the questions below to brainstorm ideas for your writing. Then share your ideas with a partner. Ask your partner for more ideas.

What do you use the two apps for? What can you do with each app?

_____

_____

Do you use the two apps a lot? Which one do you use more?

_____

_____

What is special about each app? Is there something that you can do with one app but not with the other app?

_____

_____

Are the apps easy to use? Are they well-designed? Is one better than the other?

_____

_____

Do you like the two apps? Which one do you prefer?

_____

_____

C. Use the Venn diagram to write notes about the similarities and differences
between the two apps.

App 1: _____   Both   App 2: _____

WRITE

Write five or more sentences about the two apps you wrote notes about in Part C.
Describe their similarities and differences. Add a title.

_____

_____

_____

_____

_____

_____

_____

_____

PROOFREAD AND EDIT

A. Proofread your sentences.

- Do you use *and*, *also*, *too*, and *but* correctly, adding commas when necessary?

- Do you use *can* and *can't* correctly?

- Are there any spelling mistakes?

B. Work with a partner. Share your sentences. Answer the questions in the Peer Review Form. Share your answers with your partner. Ask your partner about your sentences. Then edit them.

Peer Review Form	Yes	No
1. Does your partner write about similarities and differences between two apps?	☐	☐
2. Does your partner use *and*, *also*, *too*, and *but* correctly, with commas where they are needed?	☐	☐
3. Does your partner use *can* and *can't* correctly?	☐	☐
4. Are there any spelling mistakes? If there are, circle them.	☐	☐

⊙ Go to **MyEnglishLab** to complete grammar and vocabulary practices.

DEVELOP SOFT SKILLS

COMMUNICATING WITH INSTRUCTORS

You will sometimes need to communicate with an instructor outside of class. You can write an email or a text message when you need to ask a question or tell your instructor something. It is important to write in a respectful way.

A. Read the words and definitions. You will see these words in the text.

Glossary

communicate: talk or write to someone

find out: learn (new information)

office hours: times when an instructor is in his or her office to talk with students

syllabus: an instructor's plan for a course, with important information for students

CULTURE NOTE

In US colleges and universities, some of the instructors are professors, some are teaching assistants (or TAs), and some have other titles. Show respect by learning the names and titles of all your instructors (for example, *Professor Smith, Dr. Brown, Ms. Jones, Mr. Lee*). Some instructors will invite you to use their first names.

B. Read the text.

How to Communicate with Your Instructors

1 It is a good idea to communicate with your instructors in person. When you speak face-to-face, you can make sure the instructor understands you. You can also ask questions if you do not understand something. Sometimes you can talk to an instructor before or after class. But sometimes instructors prefer to talk to students during office hours. Find out what your instructor prefers.

2 When you cannot speak with an instructor, you can probably write an email or a text message. Again, find out what your instructor prefers.

3 To communicate with an instructor outside of class, it is important to have this information:

- the instructor's name
- where the instructor's office is
- when the instructor's office hours are
- the instructor's contact information, such as an email address or phone number

You can find this information on the course syllabus.

Writing an Email

4 1. Give your email a clear subject line so the instructor knows what the email will be about. Give details, like "ENG 104 assignment" or "Making an appointment with you."

2. Begin your message with a greeting, like "Dear Professor" or "Hello Dr. Brown."

3. Keep your message short and clear. Be polite.

4. End with a closing. Write "Thank you" and give your full name. After your name, put the name of your course if it is not in the subject line or message.

5. Check your spelling before you hit "Send."

6. When an instructor sends you an email, always reply. That way, he or she will know that you got the message.

(Continued)

Sending a Text

5 1. You do not need a greeting. Begin by giving your full name and the course you are taking.

2. Keep your message short and clear. Be polite.

3. Some instructors do not like messages in the style that we use with friends and family, like "can u call me." Instead, use this style: "Could you please call me?" Then explain. For example, write "I'm having a problem with our team project."

4. Check your spelling before you send the text.

5. When an instructor sends you a text, always reply. Your reply can be just "Thanks."

C. Read the statements about writing to college instructors. Are they true for an email, a text message, or both? Check (✓) your answers.

		Email	Text
1.	Write a subject line.	☐	☐
2.	Begin with a greeting.	☐	☐
3.	Write a short, clear, polite message.	☐	☐
4.	Give your full name and the name of the course you are taking.	☐	☐
5.	Check your spelling.	☐	☐

D. Work with a partner. Read the text message to an instructor. What problems do you see? How would you fix them? Rewrite the message on the lines.

Hey Miss, This is your student. I'm in your class. I was absent. I sick with the flu! I feel so bad! I'm sleeping a lot and eating chicken soup.

☹

My paper late, ok? Your my favorite teacher!

Ciao

_____

_____

_____

_____

_____

_____

_____

_____

_____

_____

E. Write a short email to your instructor. Write his or her real email address. Write a subject line and a short message. (For example, you can ask to make an appointment with your instructor during office hours.) Proofread and edit your message. Then exchange emails with a partner and give feedback.

From	
To	
Subject	

WHAT DID YOU LEARN?

Check (✓) the skills and vocabulary you learned. Circle the things you need to practice.

SKILLS

☐ I can recognize connections between ideas.

☐ I can use *but*, *and*, *also*, and *too* in sentences.

☐ I can use *can* for ability and possibility.

☐ I can use vocabulary for smartphone users.

☐ I can communicate with instructors.

VOCABULARY

☐ access	☐ focus on	☐ simple
☐ activity	☐ guide	☐ stream
☐ ads	☐ option	☐ tap
☐ billions	☐ review	☐ text
☐ design	☐ rule	☐ useful
☐ earbuds	☐ screen	☐ useless
☐ emoji	☐ scroll	☐ user
☐ fit		

◑ Go to **MyEnglishLab** to complete a self-assessment.

Chapter 6 | Step by Step

CHAPTER PROFILE

Businesses have to have processes—step-by-step ways to do things. That way, employees know what to do and customers know what to expect. We all follow processes at times.

This chapter is about some common processes in our lives. It is about the decisions we make and the instructions we follow—or choose *not* to follow.

You will read about

• the buyer decision process.

• returning items on an e-commerce site.

• protecting your personal information online.

You will write about creating an online account or profile.

For more about **BUSINESS AND TECHNOLOGY**, see Chapter 5.

See also [OC] **BUSINESS AND TECHNOLOGY**, Chapters 5 and 6.

OUTCOMES

• Recognize steps in a process
• Write instructions
• Use possessive adjectives
• Use tech-related phrasal verbs
• Give peer feedback

GETTING STARTED

Look at the photos. Then discuss the questions below with the class.

1. What are the man and woman doing? Describe what's happening. What's the piece of paper in the last photo?

2. Instructions (or directions) tell you how to do something. Do you usually follow instructions when you build something or cook something? How about when you travel, study, or wash clothes? Explain.

3. When do you give instructions to other people? Is it easy to do that? What's difficult about giving instructions in English?

⬆ Go to **MyEnglishLab** to complete a self-assessment.

READ

SKILL: RECOGNIZING STEPS IN A PROCESS

When you read about how something happens, or how to do something, you are reading about a **process.** There are two types of texts that describe processes.

Informational texts: These texts give you general information. When you read about how companies build their websites, or about how children learn to talk, you are reading an informational text. The writer explains how something happens.

Instructional texts: These texts tell you how to do something. If you want to learn how to cook a special food or how to create a WiFi network (a system of computers that are connected), then you read an instructional text. The writer gives you directions to follow.

Every process has **steps**, the parts of the process. The signal words in the box often introduce the steps:

first	second	third	next	then	after that	finally / last (of all)

Signal words are common in informational texts. Notice the signal words in the following paragraph:

Today, companies build websites using mobile-first design. **First**, they make a simple mobile site, called a prototype. **After that**, they test the prototype. They test it by showing it to many people and asking for their opinions. Those opinions are called user feedback. **Next**, the companies use the user feedback to make the mobile site better. **Then** they put the site online. **Finally**, they build their website for the bigger screens on desktop computers, laptops, and tablets.

The same signal words can be used in an instructional text. But in instructional texts, you will often see a numbered or bulleted list. When the text is a numbered list, it does not need signal words.

An instructional text usually has imperative statements. Notice the verbs in the following instructions:

How to Connect to WiFi

1. **Tap** the settings icon.

2. **Select** *WiFi* from the menu. You will see available WiFi networks.

3. **Choose** the name of the network that you want to join.

4. **Enter** the password for the network.

5. **Tap** *Join Network.*

REMEMBER

Complete the sentences.

1. In an informational text, you read about how _____.

2. In an instructional text, you read about how to _____.

3. Both types of texts describe a _____.

4. Signal words like *first*, *next*, and *finally* often introduce the _____ in a process.

VOCABULARY PREVIEW

A. Read the sentences. Look at the boldfaced words and phrases. Do you know what they mean? Share your ideas with a partner.

1. Companies use ads to tell you, the **consumer**, about their products.

2. I have to make a **decision** about which color phone to buy.

3. Teachers **evaluate** your learning when they give you tests.

4. Do you think people change as they **go through** life?

5. You can **look for** information about the phone online.

6. We all have a **need** for other people to talk to.

7. Some mornings I get very hungry, and I **realize** that I forgot to have breakfast.

B. Write the boldfaced words and phrases from Part A next to their definitions.

_____ 1. a choice you make after thinking about what to do

_____ 2. a strong feeling that you want or must have something

_____ 3. try to find someone or something

_____ 4. know or understand something, often for the first time, often suddenly

_____ 5. a person who buys things or uses services

_____ 6. experience (a series of events or a period of time)

_____ 7. think about how good something is

⬥ Go to **MyEnglishLab** to complete a vocabulary practice.

PREDICT

Look at the title of the text and the photo on page 124. What are two steps that you think most people take when buying a phone? Write them below.

1. _____

_____

2. _____

_____

A. Read the text. Complete the sentence after each paragraph.

The Buyer Decision Process

1 Are you thinking about buying a new phone? Maybe you have a phone, but it's old and slow. So you want a new one. You see ads for new phones, or you hear about them from friends. How do you decide which one to buy? Whether we know it or not, we all take certain steps when we decide to buy a new phone or anything else. We go through *the buyer decision process.*

1. _____ people follow the buyer decision process.

   a. All   b. Some

2 The buyer decision process has five steps. First, you, the consumer, realize that you have a problem or a need. For example, you think that your phone is old, and that's a problem for you. So you need a new phone. Second, you look for information. You look at websites, read reviews, or ask your friends. Third, you compare your options: Is a big screen or a small screen better? Should I get a black phone, a red phone, or a silver phone? Apple® or Samsung®?

2. There are _____ steps in the buyer decision process.

   a. 3   b. 5

3 After comparing options, you make a decision: You want a red phone with a big screen. You then go to the store and buy it. That is the fourth step: making a decision and buying the product. Finally, you review the product and the process. Do you like the phone? Is it easy to use? This final step is important. If you like the product, you will probably buy more products like this. And you will probably buy from the same company again. If you don't like the product, it is important to review the process. Maybe you will make changes the next time you buy something.

3. In the final step of the process, you _____ the product.

   a. buy   b. review

B. Look at the steps you wrote in Predict. Are they part of the buyer decision process?

🔊 Go to **MyEnglishLab** to reread the text.

READ AGAIN

A. Read the text again. Then complete the chart below. Look for signal words in the text to help you.

The Buyer Decision Process

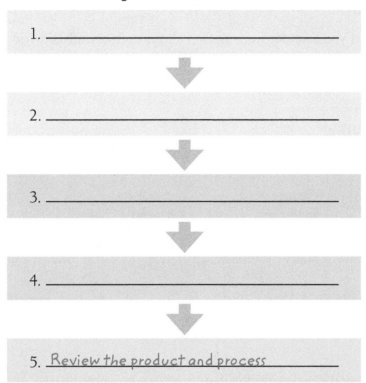

1. _____

2. _____

3. _____

4. _____

5. <u>Review the product and process</u>

B. Circle all correct answers.

1. What kind of text is "The Buyer Decision Process"?

   a. It's an informational text. It describes how something happens.

   b. It's an instructional text. It gives directions on how to do something.

   c. It's a personal story. It describes one person's shopping experience.

2. What's the main idea of the text?

   a. People should think about many things before they buy something.

   b. People have a lot of options when they decide to buy a phone.

   c. People usually follow five steps when they buy something.

3. According to the text, how do people look for information about a product?

   a. They check websites.

   b. They read reviews.

   c. They talk to their friends.

4. Why is the review stage important for the consumer?

   a. That's how you realize that you have a problem or a need.

   b. That's how you make a decision about which product is best.

   c. That's how you decide if the product you bought is right for you.

C. Think about two things that you bought recently: something small and inexpensive (like food or a pen) and something more expensive (like clothing or a phone). Then read the questions. Discuss them with a partner or in a small group.

1. What are the two things you bought? Did you have a need or a problem before buying each one? Explain.

2. Before buying, did you look for information about each thing? Did you compare your options? Explain.

3. Do you like your choices? Explain.

VOCABULARY REVIEW

Complete the sentences with the words from the box.

consumers	evaluate	look for	realize
decision	go through	need	

1. _____ have many options when they shop. Sometimes it's hard to choose what to buy.

2. Before I buy something, I _____ a process to find the best product for me.

3. Product reviews help me _____ the good things and bad things about a product.

4. I _____ the best price at different stores or websites.

5. It takes time to make a _____ about what to buy, especially if there are many options.

6. Sometimes I buy things that I have no real _____ for—I just want them!

7. Sometimes when I _____ that I don't really need something, I return it.

⬆ Go to **MyEnglishLab** to read another text.

WRITE

SKILL: WRITING INSTRUCTIONS

Instructions are common in academic life. You need to be able to give them and follow them. For example, professors sometimes give instructions in class for submitting papers (giving papers to the professor). You hear the instructions and write them down. If a friend is not in class, maybe he or she will ask you for the instructions. You can email your friend to tell him or her how to submit a paper. You give him or her the instructions.

When you give instructions, use imperative statements. Make sure that your reader can clearly understand the steps. When you write instructions in the form of a paragraph, use signal words to introduce the steps. But it is often better to use a list with numbers. See the example below.

How to Change Your Password

1. Sign in to your email.

2. Click on the Settings icon at the top right of the screen.

3. Click on the Security tab at the bottom of the screen.

4. Scroll down to the Change Password box. Click on it.

5. Type in your old password and then type in your new password.

6. Click Change Password. You can use your new password now.

REMEMBER

Circle all correct answers.

When you write instructions, _____ .

a. use imperative statements

b. be very clear

c. use numbers or signal words for each step

d. ask questions

Grammar for Writing — Using possessive adjectives

Possessive adjectives show that someone has or owns something:

I own a car. That's **my** car over there.

You have nice eyes. **Your** eyes are a beautiful blue.

Possessive adjectives replace **possessive nouns**:

her
Alexa's house is really nice. I love ~~Alexa's~~ house.

his
That's my brother's laptop. I can't use ~~my brother's~~ laptop.

A possessive adjective always comes before a noun. It does not matter if the noun is singular or plural—the possessive adjective does not change:

That's **her book**.

Those are **her books**.

Possessive Adjectives	Examples
my	**My** phone is black.
your	**Your** shirt is a nice color.
his	I really like **his** new car.
her	**Her** name is Jen.
its	This laptop is new, but **its** screen is really small.
our	Come to **our** house around 8 P.M. tonight.
their	Alex and Drew are fun, but **their** friends are boring.

GRAMMAR NOTE

Its and *it's* are different.

- *Its* is a possessive adjective:
  The company makes sneakers.
  Its *sneakers are well designed.*

- *It's* is a contraction of *it + is:*
  It's *a famous company.*

A. Circle the correct possessive adjective. Write it on the line.

1. A: Where's my phone? I can't find it.

   B: Look for it on _____ desk. You often leave it there.

   a. their   b. your   c. its

2. A: What's your password?

   B: I'm sorry, but I don't share _____ passwords with anyone.

   a. your   b. my   c. their

3. A: What do you plan to buy for your brother's birthday?

   B: I don't know. _____ digital camera doesn't work. Maybe I can get him a new one.

   a. His   b. Its   c. My

4. A: Why is that laptop so cheap?

   B: It's inexpensive because of _____ size and weight. It's too big and heavy. People don't like it.

   a. its   b. their   c. his

5. A: What grade did your sister get on the final project?

   B: I don't know yet. The professor has to evaluate _____ work.

   a. his   b. my   c. her

6. A: I don't know how to use my new smartwatch.

   B: Call Sofia and Priya, or go to _____ house. They both have smartwatches. They can help.

   a. her   b. my   c. their

7. A: How can I help you?

   B: My husband and I need to cancel _____ credit card. Someone hacked into our bank account.

   a. our   b. its   c. your

B. Use the correct possessive adjective to complete the sentences.

1. Users say it's easier to read product reviews on _____ phones than their laptops. The phone app has a simpler design.

2. My sister doesn't like the style of _____ new phone, but it takes great pictures.

3. My brother and I want to focus on improving _____ grades. We plan to do more online practice at home.

4. Add emojis to your texts. It helps people understand _____ feelings.

5. My father wants to keep _____ old desktop computer. It's slow, but it's familiar to him.

6. I use an app to track _____ diet and exercise. The technology helps me eat better and move more.

7. This is a good website, but _____ design is complicated. The app works better.

C. Read the letter. Find the five mistakes and write the correct possessive adjectives.

Dear Ms. Jones,

I need some business advice. Can you help?

I have an online business with a partner, Faisal. We sell party supplies. When customers buy ours products, they sign up and create an account. As a result, we have a lot of they personal information. Customers trust us to protect theirs credit card numbers. I agree—we must do that.

I say we need new software to update our computer system. Faisal doesn't agree. Its goal is to make money. He doesn't want to spend it.

Please tell me: What's you advice?

Thanks,

Aaron

⊙ Go to **MyEnglishLab** for more grammar practice.

WRITE INSTRUCTIONS
STEP 1: READ TO WRITE

A. Read the words and definitions. You will see these words in the text.

> **Glossary**
>
> **broken:** not working, needing to be fixed
>
> **drop-down menu:** a list of options on a website
>
> **item:** a thing, often one out of a group or set of things
>
> **label:** a piece of paper on a product or package with information about it
>
> **order:** when a customer asks a company to send a product
>
> **refund:** money that a company gives back to you because you are not happy with a product
>
> **return:** send a product back to a company

A label

B. Read the text. Answer the question after each section.

Returning an Item

1 Marci needed a new phone. So she did the usual things. She looked for phones on her favorite e-commerce site, WebShopping. She compared a few phones and compared their prices. She made a decision, placed her order, and a few days later, received her new phone. But the screen was broken. Now she needs to return the phone.

> 1. Why does Marci want to return her phone?
>
>   a. The screen is broken.
>
>   b. The screen is too small.

2 Marci checked the WebShopping site and found these instructions to return her phone:

How to Return Your Item

1. Sign in to your WebShopping account (or open the WebShopping app on your phone).

2. Click on **My Orders**. You will see a list of all your orders.

3. Find the item that you want to return. Then click on the **Return** tab next to the item.

4. From the drop-down menu, choose the reason for returning the item. Choose **I want a refund** or **Send a new item**.

5. Print the return label.

6. Put your item into a box.

7. Put the return label on the box.

8. Send the item back.

Marci is printing a label.

2. What kind of text is the list of steps on the WebShopping site?

    a. an informational text

    b. an instructional text

3 Marci took the box to the post office. She thinks that she can get a refund in a week to ten days. But she still needs a new phone. Now she has to go through the process again.

3. What does Marci want the company to do?

    a. send her a new phone

    b. pay her back the money for the phone

C. Circle the correct answer.

1. Which happened first?

    a. Marci compared the prices of phones.

    b. Marci looked for phones on WebShopping.

2. Which happened first?

    a. Marci placed her order for a phone.

    b. Marci checked WebShopping for return instructions.

3. Which step shows Marci all her past orders?

    a. Step 2

    b. Step 3

4. Which does Marci see first?

    a. a *Return* tab

    b. a drop-down menu

5. In Step 4, which option does Marci choose?

    a. *I want a refund.*

    b. *Send a new item.*

6. Which step do the instructions tell Marci to do first?

    a. Put the label on the box.

    b. Put the phone in the box.

🔊 Go to **MyEnglishLab** to reread the text.

STEP 2: PREPARE TO WRITE

We create accounts online for many reasons. For example, we create accounts for e-commerce sites. We also create user profiles for some websites, such as social media sites.

Imagine that a friend or family member wants to create a user profile or an online account. Write instructions to help him or her. Follow these steps.

1. Write the name of a website that you know. It can be a social media site, an e-commerce site, a gaming site, or something else.

   _____

2. Think about the first step in the process of creating an account or a user profile for the site. Do you go to a website? Do you download an app? Write the first step below. (If you do not know the process for the site you choose, go to the site to find out.)

   _____

3. Think about the information that you need. Do you need an email address to create the account? How about a credit card number? A password? What else? Write the kinds of information you need below.

   _____

   _____

   _____

4. If you are creating a profile, what else can you add to it? Should you have a photo? Should you have other information? Write these things below.

   _____

   _____

   _____

5. What's the last step? Write it below.

   _____

STEP 3: WRITE

Use your notes from Step 2 to write a list of instructions. Be sure to number the steps. Add any necessary details to each instruction. Write a title for your instructions (*How to … *).

   _____

_____

_____

_____

_____

_____

_____

STEP 4: PROOFREAD AND EDIT

A. Proofread your sentences.

- Do you number the steps?
- Do you use imperative statements?
- Do you use possessive adjectives correctly?
- Are there any spelling mistakes?

B. Work with a partner. Share your sentences. Answer the questions in the Peer Review Form. Share your answers with your partner. Ask your partner about your sentences. Then edit them.

Peer Review Form	Yes	No
1. Does your partner write instructions?	☐	☐
2. Are there any steps missing?	☐	☐
3. Does your partner number the steps?	☐	☐
4. Does your partner use imperatives correctly?	☐	☐
5. Does your partner use possessive adjectives correctly?	☐	☐
6. Are there any spelling mistakes? If there are, circle them.	☐	☐

C. We often give instructions by speaking. Work with a new partner. Tell your partner your instructions. Instead of numbers, use signal words like *first*, *next*, and *finally* to help your partner understand the steps. Then listen to your partner's instructions and take notes. Write the steps below.

1. _____
2. _____
3. _____
4. _____
5. _____
6. _____
7. _____
8. _____
9. _____
10. _____

D. Discuss these questions with your partner.

1. Was it easy to understand each other? Why or why not?

2. Ask your partner to check the instructions that you wrote. Is everything correct?

3. Is it easy to give instructions? What signal words help you to introduce each step?

BUILDING VOCABULARY

USING TECH-RELATED PHRASAL VERBS

There is a special type of verb in English called a **phrasal verb**. Phrasal verbs are usually made of two words, a verb + a particle (an adverb or preposition, such as *up*, *out*, *down*, or *off*). Some examples are *give up* and *work out*. Some phrasal verbs have more than one particle, such as *come up with*.

A phrasal verb has a different meaning from the verb alone. Look at the examples in the chart.

Phrasal Verb	Meaning	Example
give up	stop doing something	Lisa had to **give up** sports after she hurt her knee.
work out	exercise	I usually **work out** in the afternoons after class.
come up with	think of (a new idea)	Mohammed **comes up with** good ideas all the time.

There are many phrasal verbs related to technology. Here are some of the most common ones:

Phrasal Verb	Meaning
back up	save a copy of information from one device on another device (for safekeeping)
log in	connect to a computer system (such as a website) by using special information
set up	make ready to use (something like a computer, phone, or software)
sign in	put your name and password into a computer or website so you can use it
sign out	leave a website or account that you signed in to
sign up	give information to create an account
turn on	make a light, computer, or other electrical device start working
turn off	make a light, computer, or other electrical device stop working

> **TIP**
>
> To remember new words, write short stories using them. Stories help us remember things, even if they are very simple. For example:
>
> *After school, I go home and turn on my computer. I sign in to my email and check it. Then I sign out and play computer games. When I'm done, I turn off my computer and …*

A. Look at the chart. Can you guess how the phrasal verbs are used? Put a ✓ for the words you think can go together. Put an ✗ for words that you don't think go together.

	a phone	your email	a user account	a TV	a computer	files
back up	✓					
log in (to)	✗					
set up	✓					
sign in (to)	✗					
sign out (of)	✗					
sign up (for)	✗					
turn off	✓					
turn on	✓					

B. Use phrasal verbs to complete the sentences. Notice that sometimes an object comes between the verb and its particle.

1. If you have a new computer, you have to _____ it _____ before you can use it.

2. You should _____ your computer often so that copies of your files are safely stored in another location.

3. You must _____ for an account before you can buy anything on this website. But new accounts are easy to create.

4. Please _____ your phones _____. You can't have your phones on during the test.

5. To check your email, you have to _____ first with your user name and password.

6. Always _____ of an account when you finish using it. That helps to protect your information.

7. Do you want to watch TV? Use the power button to _____ it _____.

8. Computers at schools and libraries are locked. You must _____ with your information or a password before you can use them.

C. Take out a piece of paper. Write the eight phrasal verbs on it. Then close your book. Work with a partner. Choose one phrasal verb from the list to explain to your partner. Don't say the phrasal verb—ask your partner to guess the word that you are explaining. See the example.

A: This phrasal verb means "save or copy information."

B: I don't know. Tell me more!

A: You do this to keep the information safe, so you won't lose it if you lose your phone or your computer crashes.

B: Back up?

A: Yep, you got it. Now it's your turn.

◑ Go to MyEnglishLab to complete a vocabulary practice.

APPLY YOUR SKILLS

In this chapter, you read about instructions and processes, and you learned about the buyer decision process and the process for returning an item ordered from an e-commerce site. You also wrote instructions on how to create an account for an e-commerce site or a profile for another type of site. In Apply Your Skills, you will learn about cybersecurity: protecting your information on your mobile devices and online.

VOCABULARY PREVIEW

A. Read the sentences. Look at the boldfaced words. Do you know what they mean? Share your ideas with a partner.

1. They have to **cancel** the baseball game because it's raining.

2. **Criminals** try to take people's phones and laptops and then use them to get money.

3. Companies collect a lot of **data** about you, like your name, your age, the things you buy, and the places you go.

4. I never **delete** my emails. That's why I have thousands of them in my inbox!

5. Paulo gets really good grades, **especially** in math and English.

6. I don't want anyone to **hack** my phone and get my personal information.

7. You don't want other people to access your files, so **lock** your computer. Then no one else can get in.

8. Protect your phone! People can **steal** it and sell it to someone else.

B. Write the boldfaced words from Part A next to their definitions.

_____ 1. remove (information, like files from a computer or words from a text)

_____ 2. close something so that other people cannot open it

_____ 3. used to show one thing is more important than others

_____ 4. stop something from continuing, or stop it from happening

_____ 5. people who do bad things that are against the law

_____ 6. information

_____ 7. take something from someone else without asking

He's stealing her phone.

_____ 8. get information from someone's computer or phone without the person knowing about it, also *hack into*

🔊 Go to **MyEnglishLab** to complete a vocabulary practice.

PREDICT

Privacy (keeping your information safe from others) is important. How do you keep the information on your phone safe? How do you protect your privacy? Check (✓) all your answers.

☐ I use passwords for my phone.

☐ I must enter a password before I can use my apps.

☐ I don't use social media.

☐ I don't share much information on social media sites.

☐ I sign out of my email and other accounts when I finish using them.

☐ I don't use WiFi outside of my home and school.

READ

A. Read the text. Answer the question after each paragraph.

TechNow   YOUR VIEW   WORLD VIEW   CONNECT   MORE

I Got Hacked—Protect Yourself!

1 Somebody hacked my online account for the WebShopping site a few months ago—what a terrible experience! They stole my credit card number and my social security number. With that information, they signed up for at least three new credit cards in my name. But luckily, WebShopping learned about the problem and emailed me about it. After many hours on the phone, I canceled all my credit cards and fixed the problem. I don't want to get hacked again, and I don't want you to get hacked. So here are a few tips for protecting your privacy.

  1. Which statement is true?

    a. The writer works for a company called WebShopping.

    b. The writer wants to help people to protect their personal information.

(Continued)

CULTURE NOTE

In the United States, a social security number is a nine-digit number that people get from the government. The number is used for work, taxes, bank accounts, and other important things.

2 Many people get hacked because their phones get stolen. If a criminal steals a phone, he or she can use the information on it. So remember to:

- Always keep your phone locked when you aren't using it.

- Use an app to lock your apps, especially the apps with your most important data. There are many app-locker apps that you can download to your phone.

- Don't leave your phone in a public place, like at the library or a café. Someone can steal it.

2. How can you keep the information on your phone safe?

a. Download and use an app-locker app.

b. Don't use your phone at a café.

3 Hackers (people who hack) can access information on your phone even when it's in your hand. So remember these tips:

- Use only safe WiFi networks, like the network in your home or school. Free WiFi networks can be dangerous.

- Turn off your Bluetooth when you're not using it. You may not know this, but Bluetooth is an easy way for hackers to access your phone.

Bluetooth icon

3. Which of these instructions will help protect you from hackers?

a. Don't use free WiFi networks.

b. Don't turn off your Bluetooth.

4 Companies you do business with have a lot of your data. Hackers can steal your data from them. So protect yourself:

- Change your privacy settings in your email, social media, and other apps. Make them safe by sharing less of your personal information. Don't let companies know your location.

- Delete accounts that you don't use.

- Use unique passwords and change them often. Don't use your name in passwords or use passwords like *Password1*.

4. Which of these actions can be dangerous?

a. deleting accounts

b. sharing information about yourself in apps

5 Nothing can protect you and your data 100 percent of the time. But by following these tips, you can make it harder for hackers and other criminals to steal your information. The harder it is for them, the safer your data will be.

5. What will happen if you follow the writer's instructions?

   a. Your personal information will be better protected.

   b. Your personal information will always be safe.

B. Look again at your answers to the question "How do you protect your privacy?" in Predict. Do you want to change any of them?

🔾 Go to **MyEnglishLab** to reread the text.

READ AGAIN

A. Read the text again. Then read the statements below. Circle *T* (true) or *F* (false). Correct the false statements.

T / F 1. A hacker stole the writer's bank information.

T / F 2. The writer can't fix the problem.

T / F 3. Criminals can steal your phone and take your information from it.

T / F 4. Use an app-locker app to keep other people from using your apps.

T / F 5. Hackers can get information on your phone through Bluetooth.

T / F 6. You should delete old accounts that you don't use.

T / F 7. Following the eight tips in the text will protect your data all the time.

B. Work with a partner. Imagine that your parents or grandparents come to you and say, "Tell us how to protect our data and privacy from hackers." Use the information in the reading to give them five instructions. Think: Which tips are the most important? Write your instructions with your partner.

1. _____

2. _____

3. _____

4. _____

5. _____

C. Share your instructions with another pair of students. Are your instructions the same as or different from theirs? Explain the reasons for your choices.

VOCABULARY REVIEW

Complete the sentences with the words from the box.

cancel	data	especially	lock
criminals	delete	hack	steal

1. It can be easy for people to _____ into computers and personal devices, so be careful.

2. Hackers want to _____ your private financial, health, and social information. Then they can use it for the wrong reasons.

3. It's important to protect your personal _____ from computer hackers.

4. Hackers sometimes _____ information from a person's computer, so he or she loses it all.

5. It's hard for the police to stop these _____.

6. Keep your information safe. Always _____ your devices with strong passwords.

7. It's _____ helpful to use two ways to log into a site, like a password and a code from a text message.

8. If someone hacks into your credit card account, call the credit card company and _____ the card immediately.

THINK VISUALLY

Look at the pie chart and discuss the questions.

1. A data breach is when a business or other organization fails to protect its data from hackers. The pie chart shows the five categories of data breaches in the United States in 2018 and the percentage of data breaches for each category. Describe the chart. Does any of the information surprise you? Why or not?

Percentage of Data Breaches by Category in the United States, 2018

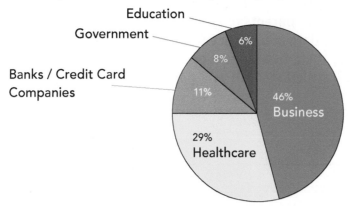

2. Think about the data in each category. What do hackers want to steal from these types of organizations? What information is most valuable in each type of data breach?

GRAMMAR

USING POSSESSIVE ADJECTIVES

Use the correct possessive adjectives to complete the sentences in the second email.

From	gkh1424@therewegoagain.com
To	mrbusiness@usefultips.com
Subject	Advice, please

Dear Mr. Business,

I fix computers and smartphones at home. I need more customers, so I want to advertise online. How do I start?

Thanks,

Gerry

From	mrbusiness@usefultips.com
To	gkh1424@therewegoagain.com
Subject	Re: Advice, please

Hi Gerry,

That's a good question. First, talk to people that live in (1) _____ city. Ask them about problems they have with (2) _____ devices. Next, write a description of (3) _____ business and take pictures of the types of devices you fix. After that, open an account on social media and upload (4) _____ pictures on a new page. Use it to create an ad for your business. Make sure (5) _____ design is simple and easy to understand. Then invite (6) _____ friends and customers to "like" your page. Contact people who write popular blogs. Ask them to include your page on (7) _____ websites.

I hope (8) _____ tips help you!

ASSIGNMENT

Choose a process and write instructions.

PREPARE TO WRITE

A. Read the questions. Brainstorm ideas for your writing.

1. Think about a normal day in your life. What do you do in the morning? Afternoon? Evening? Write notes about your day below.

_____

_____

_____

_____

_____

2. Of the things that you do during the day, which ones have processes? For example, you might follow a process when you make coffee, cook rice, or start a car. Write a few ideas below.

_____   _____

_____   _____

_____   _____

3. Look at your ideas from Step 2. Choose one process that you can write instructions for, and write notes about it below. Follow the example. You do not have to write full sentences.

Process: How to Make Coffee

First step: Get the right amount of coffee.

Next steps: Put the coffee into the coffee maker's filter.

                Pour water into the coffee maker.

                Turn on the coffee maker.

Final step: Pour the coffee into a cup, and drink it.

Process: _____

First step: _____

Next steps: _____

_____

_____

_____

_____

Final step: _____

B. Work with a partner. Explain your instructions to him or her. Use signal words (like *first, second,* and *finally*) when explaining your instructions. Then listen to your partner's instructions. Consider the following questions while you listen. Share your ideas after your partner is finished.

1. What are the instructions for?

2. Are they easy to understand?

3. Does your partner clearly signal the steps with signal words?

4. Did your partner forget any steps? Should he or she add anything?

WRITE

Write your instructions in a list. Write a title on the first line. Then write one instruction on each line below. Use numbers or signal words to show the different steps.

_____

_____

_____

_____

_____

_____

_____

PROOFREAD AND EDIT

A. Proofread your sentences.

- Do you use imperative statements and / or signal words correctly?

- Do you use possessive adjectives correctly?

- Are there any spelling mistakes?

B. Work with a different partner. Share your sentences. Answer the questions in the Peer Review Form. Share your answers with your new partner. Ask your partner about your sentences. Then edit them.

Peer Review Form	Yes	No
1. Does your partner write instructions about a process?	☐	☐
2. Are the instructions clear and complete?	☐	☐
3. Does your partner use imperative statements correctly?	☐	☐
4. Does your partner use signal words correctly?	☐	☐
5. Are there any spelling mistakes? If there are, circle them.	☐	☐

🔊 Go to **MyEnglishLab** to complete grammar and vocabulary practices.

DEVELOP SOFT SKILLS

GIVING PEER FEEDBACK

Professors give students grades on their written work, and they usually give students feedback, too. But they are not the only ones. You, too, as a student, will sometimes have to give feedback on a classmate's written work. Reading the work of your peers (other students) and giving them feedback is a helpful part of the writing process—for them and for you.

A. Read the words and definitions. You will see these words in the text.

> ### Glossary
>
> **complimenting:** saying something nice to a person to make him or her feel good
>
> **content:** the ideas and information in a piece of writing
>
> **exchange:** give something to and get something from another person
>
> **mark the paper:** write or draw on another writer's paper
>
> **missing:** not in the place where it should be

B. Read the text.

Peer Feedback: How and Why We Give It

How to Give Peer Feedback

1 Sometimes an instructor will tell students to give peer feedback during class. You find a partner, exchange papers, and read your partner's work. Your instructor tells you what to look for. Maybe you follow the instructions in a peer review worksheet (like the Peer Review Form on page 143). It says what to look for and helps you talk with your partner.

2 You can also give peer feedback outside of class. Do you have a classmate who wants help with an assignment? Follow these steps:

   1. Read the whole paper. Think about the content. Is there enough information, or do you want the writer to say more?

   2. Read again, this time with a pencil in your hand. <u>Underline</u> any sentences that you do not understand.

   3. Read again, pencil still in hand. Mark any problems you see. You can circle words, write question marks (?), and put arrows (➔) on the paper.

3 Then it is time to talk to your partner. Follow these steps:

   1. Start by complimenting the paper. Say something like "Nice work!" or "I liked reading about _____."

   2. Ask your partner about parts of the paper that you did not understand or about information that was missing.

3. Explain the marks you made on the paper.

4. Thank your partner for showing you his or her work.

Why Give Peer Feedback?

4 Why should you give peer feedback? One reason is to help another student. Another reason is to help *yourself*! Reading other writers' work, and thinking about it, will help you become a better writer. That is because giving feedback makes you think about:

- putting ideas in the correct order.

- making information clear to a reader.

- deciding how much information a reader needs.

- looking for problems with, for example, spelling, verb forms, and word order.

5 It is usually easier to find problems in another person's paper than in your own paper. If you practice finding other people's mistakes, you will get better at finding your own.

C. Put the steps in order. Write the numbers 1–3 on the lines.

1. Working on your partner's paper

_____ a. Use a pencil to mark any problems you see on the paper.

_____ b. Read the paper and underline parts that are not clear.

_____ c. Read the paper without making any marks on it.

2. Talking with your partner

_____ a. Explain the marks you made on your partner's paper.

_____ b. Ask your partner questions.

_____ c. Say thank you to your partner.

D. Read the questions. Discuss them with a partner or in a small group.

1. When do you give and get peer feedback in your classes? When do you give and get peer feedback outside of class? Do you ever get peer feedback on papers you write in your first language?

2. What parts of giving and getting peer feedback do you like? What parts do you not like? Explain.

3. In Paragraph 4, you read, "Why should you give peer feedback? … to help *yourself!*" Do you agree? Explain.

E. Prepare to give peer feedback outside of class. Read the questions and write your answers.

1. You want to exchange papers with a classmate and share feedback. What can you say?

   _____

2. You want to compliment your partner's paper. What can you say?

   _____

3. Something in your partner's paper is not clear. What can you say?

   _____

WHAT DID YOU LEARN?

Check (✓) the skills and vocabulary you learned. Circle the things you need to practice.

SKILLS

☐ I can recognize steps in a process.

☐ I can write instructions.

☐ I can use possessive adjectives.

☐ I can use tech-related phrasal verbs.

☐ I can give peer feedback.

VOCABULARY

☐ back up	☐ evaluate	☐ realize
☐ broken	☐ go through	☐ refund
☐ cancel	☐ hack (into)	☐ return
☐ consumer	☐ item	☐ set up
☐ criminal	☐ label	☐ sign in (to)
☐ data	☐ lock	☐ sign out (of)
☐ decision	☐ log in (to)	☐ sign up (for)
☐ delete	☐ look for	☐ steal
☐ drop-down menu	☐ need	☐ turn off
☐ especially	☐ order	☐ turn on

🔊 Go to **MyEnglishLab** to complete a self-assessment.

🔊 Go to **MyEnglishLab** for a challenge reading about Business and Technology.

Psychology

Go to **MyEnglishLab** to see an introduction about **PSYCHOLOGY.**

Chapter 7 Get into the Routine

CHAPTER PROFILE

Psychology is the study of our thoughts, feelings, and actions. A person who studies how people think, feel, and behave is a **psychologist**.

This chapter is about people's daily routines—the things they do every day.

You will read about

- sleeping enough.

- the routines of Olympic swimmers.

- a pilot's routine.

You will write about your daily routine and another student's routine.

For more about **PSYCHOLOGY**, see Chapter 8. See also [OC] **PSYCHOLOGY**, Chapters 7 and 8.

OUTCOMES

- Understand numbers in a text
- Connect ideas between sentences
- Use adverbs of frequency and *every*
- Use vocabulary for daily activities
- Make healthy choices

GETTING STARTED

Read the questions. Discuss them with a partner or in a small group.

1. Look at the photo. What is she doing? How does she feel?

2. Do you have a lot of energy in the morning? What do you do after getting up? Explain.

3. Are you a night person? Do you like to stay up until 1 or 2 A.M.? How many hours do you sleep at night? Explain.

◔ Go to **MyEnglishLab** to complete a self-assessment.

READ

SKILL: UNDERSTANDING NUMBERS IN A TEXT

Academic texts, especially in the sciences, can have a lot of numbers. They are used to give information about amounts. Amounts are sometimes expressed as an **average**, a **range**, a **percentage**, or a **fraction**.

Understanding numbers can help you better understand the ideas in a text.

> **Glossary**
>
> **an average:** a number you get when you add several amounts together and divide by the number of amounts: *The average of 1, 5, and 6 is 4 because you add 1 + 5 + 6 and divide by 3.*
>
> **a range:** a set of numbers or amounts with a lower and an upper limit: *The range of ages in the class was 18 to 24.*

Look at the chart. Notice the numbers. Notice the expressions that are used with them.

AMOUNTS		
Things We Measure	**Units of Measurement**	**Examples**
Time, age	years hours minutes	Few students sleep for more than **10 hours** at night. I exercise for **30 minutes** every day.
Size, weight, height	pounds feet meters	Michael weighs **160 pounds**. The apartment building is about **600 feet** tall.
Distance	miles kilometers	My house is **10 miles** from here. The distance between New York and London is **5,585 kilometers**.
Expressions Used to Describe Amounts		**Examples**
Averages	on average an average of	Americans drink 1.6 cups of coffee **on average** every day. Americans drink **an average of** 1.6 cups of coffee a day.
Ranges	20 to 30 20–30	You should exercise for **20 to 30** minutes every day. You should get **20–30** minutes of exercise every day.
Percentages	30 percent (30%)	**Thirty percent** of students don't exercise regularly.
Fractions	one in three one third (1/3, ⅓)	Nearly **one in three** US students doesn't get regular exercise.

There are two common question forms that ask for amounts. Recognizing them will help you with tests and assignments.

QUESTIONS ABOUT AMOUNTS

Wh- Words	Question	Answer
How many	**How many** hours do students sleep at night?	Most sleep for **7–9 hours** per night.
How much	**How much** time do people spend sleeping every night?	They spend **an average of 7 hours** sleeping every night.
What percentage of	**What percentage** of students exercise regularly?	**Seventy percent** of students exercise regularly.

CULTURE NOTE

In the United States and some other English-speaking countries, people measure height in feet and weight in pounds: 1 foot = 0.305 meters; 1 pound = 0.454 kilograms.

GRAMMAR NOTE

Questions with *how many* and *how much* ask for information about a quantity. *How many* asks about countable nouns, like *hours*, *days*, and *years*. *How much* is for noncount nouns, like *time* or *sleep*.

REMEMBER

Complete the sentences.

1. We use numbers to measure things like time, _____, and _____.

2. We can express amounts using averages, _____, and _____ or _____.

VOCABULARY PREVIEW

A. Read the sentences. Look at the boldfaced words and phrases. Do you know what they mean? Share your ideas with a partner.

1. There was a car **accident** in front of my house. One person was hurt and went to the hospital.

2. Children learn from other children and from **adults**, like their parents and teachers.

3. The **average** American drinks one or two cups of coffee a day.

4. Don't text and drive: It's **dangerous**!

5. I get five hours of sleep every night. That's clearly not **enough** sleep because I'm always tired.

6. Kenta **falls asleep** during movies. He can't stay awake.

7. Joaquín likes to listen to music **while** he studies.

Listening **while** studying

B. Write the boldfaced words and phrases from Part A next to their definitions.

_____ 1. people over 18 years old

_____ 2. when someone is hurt or something is damaged by a mistake

_____ 3. starts to sleep

_____ 4. the right amount of something; as much as you need or want

_____ 5. at the same time as

_____ 6. not safe

_____ 7. typical, usual, like most other people or things of its kind

⬆ Go to **MyEnglishLab** to complete a vocabulary practice.

PREDICT

Look at the title and photos. What kinds of numbers do you think you will you see in the text? Check (✓) your ideas.

☐ years   ☐ averages

☐ dates   ☐ ranges

☐ hours   ☐ percentages

☐ minutes   ☐ fractions

READ

A. Read the text and answer the question after each paragraph.

Sleep: Make Sure You Get Enough

1 Everybody sleeps. It's part of our daily routine. Some people sleep for 3 hours. Some people sleep for 10 hours. How much sleep is enough? Are there problems when we don't sleep enough? Scientists are trying to answer these questions.

   1. How many hours do people sleep?

      a. Most people sleep for 10 hours.

      b. People sleep for different amounts of time.

(Continued)

2 How much sleep do we need? The answer is different for people of different ages. Young children (1–5 years old) need to spend at least 40 percent of their time sleeping: 10 to 14 hours every day. School-age children (6–12 years old) need 9 to 12 hours of sleep, and teenagers (13–19 years old) need 8 to 10 hours. Adults should get about 7 to 9 hours, but older adults (65 and older) need a little less. However, the average adult gets just 6.8 hours of sleep, and many get fewer than 6 hours.

2. How many hours of sleep do most adults need?

a. about 7–9 hours

b. about 8–10 hours

3 One in three adults in the United States is sleep-deprived (does not get enough sleep at night), and this can be dangerous. One danger is falling asleep while driving. According to a government study, in 2013, sleepy driving was the reason for more than 70,000 accidents. The government says that people died in about 8 percent of these accidents. Being tired also makes it difficult to learn and remember new things. And, as we all know, when people don't sleep enough, they can become angry easily. So make sure you get enough sleep.

3. In 2013, what percentage of sleepy driving accidents were deadly?

a. about 8 percent

b. more than 70,000

B. Look at your predictions again. Were they correct?

Go to **MyEnglishLab** to reread the text.

READ AGAIN

A. Read the text again. Then complete the sentences with numbers.

1. Some people sleep for only _____ hours every night. Others sleep for 10 hours.

2. Young children should spend _____ percent of their time asleep.

3. If a child is ten years old, he or she needs _____ hours of sleep.

4. Teenagers are people who are _____ years old.

5. Teenagers need _____ hours of sleep every night.

6. On average, adults get _____ hours of sleep per night.

7. In 2013, there were more than _____ sleepy driving accidents.

B. Draw a line to connect each paragraph with its main idea.

1. Paragraph 1   a. There are problems with not sleeping enough.
2. Paragraph 2   b. Sleep needs are different at different ages.
3. Paragraph 3   c. Sleep is something that we all do differently.

C. Complete the sentences.

1. I usually sleep _____ hours per night.
2. I want to sleep _____ hours per night.

D. Read the questions. Discuss them with a partner.

1. Look at the information in Paragraph 2. Do you sleep enough? Do you want to sleep more? Explain.

2. When you don't sleep enough at night, are you different the next day? Do you make more mistakes? Do you forget things easily? Do you get angry easily? Explain.

3. Is it easy to find and understand numbers in a text? Why or why not?

VOCABULARY REVIEW

Complete the sentences with the words and phrases from the box.

accident	average	enough	while
adults	dangerous	fall asleep	

1. Reggie is still hungry. He didn't eat _____.
2. _____ you are driving, focus on the road and the other drivers.
3. In the past, many people died on long boat trips. The trips were _____.
4. Many people were hurt in the _____.
5. Children need more sleep than _____.
6. Train trips are so boring. I _____ on trains sometimes.
7. The _____ adult needs less sleep than a child or a teenager.

⬣ Go to **MyEnglishLab** to read another text.

WRITE

SKILL: CONNECTING IDEAS BETWEEN SENTENCES

A sentence expresses a simple idea about a topic. To say more about a topic, you can write a **paragraph**. A paragraph is a group of sentences that work together to express a bigger idea—a main idea.

TIP

A paragraph is not a list of sentences. It looks different. When you write a paragraph, begin each new sentence right after the sentence before it, on the same line.

Connecting the ideas in a paragraph is important. Well-connected sentences make your ideas easier to understand. In a paragraph about a series of events, use time signal words to show the order of events. Look at the example and notice the boldfaced words.

> Kai does the same things every weekday morning. He wakes up at 7 A.M. He brushes his teeth, **and then** he takes a shower. **After his shower,** he eats breakfast. **Then** he leaves for work. He usually takes the bus, but he takes his bike when the weather is nice. He gets to work **at 9:15, and then** he starts his workday.

The paragraph about Kai's routine is easy to understand for these reasons:

1. The subject (*Kai*, or *he*) is the same throughout the paragraph.

2. The events are connected to each other in order.

3. The time markers and the signal words, like *then* and *after*, guide the reader, showing the order of events. For example, notice that after *takes a shower,* you find *After his shower.* The writer uses *After his shower* to clearly connect the events in the two sentences.

Study the chart.

	Example	Order of Events
then	She showers. **Then** she eats breakfast	1. She showers. 2. She eats breakfast.
before + noun	**Before class**, I always have a cup of coffee.	1. I have coffee. 2. Class starts.
after + noun	**After work**, I exercise.	1. Work finishes. 2. I exercise.
finally	She reads a book in bed. **Finally,** around 11 P.M., she falls asleep.	1. She reads. 2. She falls asleep.

REMEMBER

Complete the sentences.

1. You must make your writing _____ to understand.

2. Connect ideas and events by using signal words like *then* and *next*. You can also use the words _____ and _____ + a noun to show the order of events.

Grammar for Writing Using adverbs of frequency and *every*

Adverbs of Frequency

We use **adverbs of frequency** to tell how often something happens. Common adverbs of frequency are *always*, *usually*, *often*, *sometimes*, and *never*.

Adverbs of frequency follow special rules. Study the chart to see where adverbs of frequency go in sentences.

100% of the time / happens all the time

always

usually

often

sometimes

never

0% of the time / doesn't happen

	THE ADVERBS *ALWAYS*, *USUALLY*, *OFTEN*, *SOMETIMES*, AND *NEVER*	
	Rules	**Examples**
1.	In sentences with the verb *be*, the adverb comes after *be*.	Classes <u>are</u> **always** between 9 A.M. and 6 P.M. Brent <u>is</u> **never** late for work.
2.	With other verbs, the adverb comes before the verb.	Lee **always** <u>eats</u> breakfast in the morning. Ji-Eun **usually** <u>goes</u> to bed at 11 P.M. Paul **never** <u>studies</u> for tests.
3.	The adverbs *usually*, *often*, and *sometimes* can also come at the beginning of a sentence. Do not use *always* or *never* at the beginning of a sentence.	**Usually** **Sometimes** I meet my friends after work. **Often**

Every

We also use ***every*** to say how often something happens. We use it for events that happen regularly.

Every Wednesday, Wenjing goes to a dance lesson.

Study the rules and examples in the chart.

	EVERY	
	Rules	**Examples**
1.	Use *every* + a noun that describes a period of time.	Kara goes to the library **every** <u>night</u>. Take the medicine once **every** <u>8 hours</u>.
2.	A phrase with *every* can go at the beginning or end of a sentence.	**Every** <u>night</u>, Kara goes to the library. Wenjing goes to a dance lesson **every** <u>Wednesday</u>.

GRAMMAR NOTE

Use *how often* to ask about events that happen repeatedly.

A: **How often** do you go to the movies?

B: I go almost every weekend.

REMEMBER

Complete the sentences.

1. The adverbs _____ , _____ , and _____ can come at the beginning of a sentence.

2. The adverbs _____ and _____ must come next to the verb.

3. Use _____ + noun to show that something happens regularly.

A. Put the words in the correct order.

1. around 8 A.M. / My mom / wakes up / often

   _____

2. at 10 A.M. / My brother / usually / and I / get up

   _____

3. always / We / are / hungry / in the morning

   _____

4. Our family / eats / on Saturdays / never / breakfast at home

   _____

5. we go to / our favorite / Every / restaurant / Saturday

   _____

6. grandparents / our / we / Sometimes / also invite

   _____

7. do you / often / for breakfast / How / go out

   _____

B. Circle the correct answers.

1. How **often / usually** do you go to the gym during the week?
2. Sheryl **often / never** exercises. She says that she doesn't have time.
3. **Sometimes / Always** Paul goes running after work. Other days, he plays basketball outside.
4. Tim **usually / always** goes swimming after he finishes classes. He never misses a day.
5. Asma and Ayesha **never / usually** walk home after school. But on Tuesdays, they take the bus.
6. **Every / Sometimes** Monday and Wednesday night, Ismael and his team play football.

C. Look at Samuel's schedule and read the paragraph about him. Find and correct the five mistakes with adverbs of frequency and *every*.

	Sunday	Monday	Tuesday	Wednesday	Thursday	Friday	Saturday
Work		X	X	X	X	X	
Math class		X		X			
English class		X		X			
Study	X		X		X	X	X
Exercise	X	X	X	X	X	X	X

Samuel usually is busy. He works and takes classes at the university. He often works five days a week. Sometimes he works on weekends. Always Monday and Wednesday he takes math and English classes. When he doesn't have classes, he studies. He never goes to the gym to exercise.

➊ Go to **MyEnglishLab** for more grammar practice.

WRITE ABOUT YOUR ROUTINE

STEP 1: READ TO WRITE

A. Read the words and definitions. You will see these words in the text.

Glossary

calorie: a measure of the amount of energy in food

competition: an event where athletes or teams play against each other

gym: a place to exercise

nap: a short sleep during the daytime

wake up: stop sleeping

B. Read the text. Follow the instructions after Paragraphs 1–3.

Everyday Routines: Olympic Swimmers

1 Olympic swimmers start their day early. Most wake up at around 6:30 A.M. and eat a really big breakfast. Next, they go to the pool and swim for a few hours. After swimming, they eat a big lunch. In fact, Olympic swimmers eat more than 10,000 calories a day. Compared to most Americans, this is a lot. The average American eats about 3,500 calories a day.

An Olympic swimmer in a pool

> 1. Underline the words and phrases that show order of events. (*Hint: There are two.*)

2 In the afternoon, many swimmers take a nap. After napping, they go to the gym to—you guessed it!—exercise some more. Amazingly, the average Olympic swimmer exercises 4–6 hours every day.

> 2. Underline the phrase that shows order of events.

3 At night, they swim for another hour or two and then eat a big dinner. Finally, after a long day of exercise, they go to sleep between 10 and 11 P.M. In all, Olympic swimmers sleep 9–10 hours a day.

> 3. Underline the words and phrases that show order of events. (*Hint: There are three.*)

4 Olympic swimmers need a lot of food, exercise, and sleep. Their daily routines make their bodies strong and prepare them well for their competitions.

C. Read the list of events in the day of an average Olympic swimmer. Then put them in the correct order (1–9).

CULTURE NOTE

Most doctors say that men should eat about 2,300 calories per day and that women should eat about 1,800.

_____ swims 3–4 hours

_____ eats lunch

__1__ wakes up at 6:30 A.M.

_____ goes to the gym

_____ eats breakfast

__9__ goes to bed around 10–11 P.M.

_____ eats dinner

_____ swims 1–2 hours

_____ takes a nap

○ Go to **MyEnglishLab** to reread the text.

STEP 2: PREPARE TO WRITE

A. Read the questions. Discuss them with a partner or in a small group.

1. Do you have a morning routine? That is, do you have a routine between waking up and leaving your home? Describe it.

2. Do you have routines at school or work? Describe your usual routine for one day.

3. Do you have a nighttime routine? That is, do you have a routine between coming home and going to bed? Describe it.

4. Do you have any other routines? Maybe a study routine or an exercise routine? Describe it.

B. Write notes about a routine you follow.

My Routine	
Time	Event

STEP 3: WRITE

Write a paragraph of 5 or more sentences about a routine of yours. Follow these instructions:

- Do not include the times of everything that you do. Use time signal words like _then_, _before_, and _after_ to connect the ideas.

- Use adverbs of frequency and *every* to describe how often events happen.
- Begin your paragraph with a sentence that introduces your topic. Look at these examples:

    I have a simple morning routine.

    I do the same things every Friday night.

    Here is my weekday routine.

- Give your paragraph a title.

Remember that a paragraph is not a list of sentences. Begin each new sentence on the same line as the sentence before it.

_____

_____

_____

_____

_____

_____

STEP 4: PROOFREAD AND EDIT

A. Proofread your paragraph.

- Do you focus on one topic (your routine) in your writing?
- Do you use words that show order (for example, *before, then,* and *next*)?
- Do you use adverbs of frequency? Do you use *every*?
- Are there any spelling mistakes?

B. Work with your partner. Share your paragraphs. Answer the questions in the Peer Review Form. Share feedback. Then edit your sentences.

Peer Review Form	Yes	No
1. Does your partner write about his or her routine in a clear way?	☐	☐
2. Does your partner focus on one topic in his or her writing?	☐	☐
3. Does your partner use words that show order?	☐	☐
4. Are the sentences in the form of a paragraph?	☐	☐
5. Are there any spelling mistakes? If there are, circle them.	☐	☐

C. Read the questions. Discuss them with a partner.

1. What is interesting about your partner's routine? Is your partner's routine similar to a routine you follow? Explain.

2. Was it easy to understand your partner's routine? How did time signal words help you to understand your partner's paragraph?

BUILDING VOCABULARY

USING VOCABULARY FOR DAILY ACTIVITIES

There are many activities that we do every day. For many of these—including team sports, instruments, and video games—we use the verb *play* + the activity.

He **plays basketball** every day.

They like to **play soccer**.

He is **playing baseball**.

They **play video games** together at night.

He loves to **play the guitar**.

She is very good at **playing the piano**.

For some activities—including martial arts (for example, taekwondo and karate)—we use *do* + the activity.

They are **doing taekwondo**.

She **does yoga** four times a week.

For other activities, we use *go* + **verb** + *-ing*.

She **goes running** before work every day.

He **goes swimming** after class on Tuesdays and Thursdays.

Finally, the most common way to say *spend time (with friends)* is **hang out**.

> **CULTURE NOTE**
>
> We do not say that adults "play" with friends. *Play* is used for children, as in: *Children often **play with friends** after school.*

They **hang out** between classes.

A. Circle the correct verb to complete each sentence.

1. Ben likes to **play / do / go** yoga every morning before work.

2. Aisha and Sara **play / do / go** video games together every night.

3. What time do you want to **play / do / go** running? I'm free after 6 P.M.

4. Rob is really good at **playing / doing / going** the saxophone.

5. My brother **plays / does / goes** basketball every weekend.

6. I love to **play / do / go** swimming at the beach.

7. Zoe is in a band. She **plays / does / goes** the drums.

8. Do you **play / do / go** any instruments?

He's playing the saxophone.

She's playing the drums.

B. Circle the words that are true for you.

1. I **can / can't** play an instrument.

2. I **like / don't like** to hang out with friends.

3. I **can / can't** do taekwondo.

4. I **play / don't play** basketball.

5. I **like / don't like** to go running.

6. I **like / don't like** to play video games.

C. Work with a partner or in a small group. Share your answers from Part B. Then discuss the questions.

1. What instrument can you play? What instrument do you want to play?

2. Do you like to play any sports? What sports do you like? Do you prefer to watch sports? Which ones?

3. Do you play video games at home or someplace else? Who do you play with? Which games do you like to play?

4. Do you hang out with friends every day? If not, how often do you hang out with friends? What do you usually do with your friends?

🔊 Go to **MyEnglishLab** to complete a vocabulary practice.

APPLY YOUR SKILLS

In this chapter, you read about getting enough sleep and the routines of Olympic swimmers. You wrote about a routine. In Apply Your Skills, you will learn about airplane pilots: their job and some of their routines. You will interview another student and write a paragraph about his or her routine.

VOCABULARY PREVIEW

A. Read the sentences. Look at the boldfaced words. Do you know what they mean? Share your ideas with a partner.

1. The plane's **departure** is scheduled for 8:15. It's 8:00, so we have to run!

2. There are no **flights** to Miami today because the weather there is very bad.

3. Paul goes to the gym **immediately** after work every day.

4. I hate flying. I feel much better after the plane **lands**.

5. My **pay** is great! I get lots of money from my job.

6. Doctors and nurses receive years of **training** before they can start working.

B. Write the boldfaced words from Part A next to their definitions.

_____ 1. arrives on the ground from the air

_____ 2. the money you get for doing a job

_____ 3. when a plane or train leaves a place

_____ 4. the experience of learning information and processes for a job

_____ 5. plane trips

_____ 6. right away, without waiting

○ Go to **MyEnglishLab** to complete a vocabulary practice.

PREDICT

Look at the title of the blog and the three subheadings on the next page. Think about what they mean. Then write the subheading where you think you will find this information:

The Job 1. details about training

_____ 2. getting ready for takeoff

_____ 3. how much pilots work every month

_____ 4. information about pay

_____ 5. landing the plane

_____ 6. things pilots don't like about the job

READ

A. Read the words and definitions. You will see these words in the text.

> **Glossary**
>
> **airport security:** the area set up to check people and their bags, to keep air travel safe
>
> **autopilot:** the computer that a pilot can turn on to fly a plane
>
> **first officer:** a pilot who helps the pilot in control of a plane, a copilot
>
> **flight attendants:** the people who help the passengers on a plane
>
> **jet lag:** a tired, confused feeling after a long flight

An airplane taking off

B. Read the blog post by a travel writer. Complete the sentence after each paragraph.

Tim's Travel Blog, Post #24

What's it like to live a pilot's life?

1 I live in New York, and when I have free time, I love to travel. I've traveled all over Europe, East Asia, and the Middle East. The flight from New York to Rome is 7+ hours. The flight from New York to Shanghai is 15 hours! That's a really long flight, and it's hard to do. I had jet lag for almost a week. But when I fly, I usually just get on the plane, watch a movie, and then fall asleep. How do the pilots do it? Is it tiring? Do they get jet lag, too?

VOCABULARY NOTE

The symbol + is called *a plus sign*. When you read "2 + 2," you say "two plus two" and you add the numbers together.

A plus sign after a number means "or more." When you read "7+ hours," you say "seven-plus hours" and it means "7 or more hours" or "at least 7 hours."

1. The flight from New York to Shanghai is _____ long.

The Job

2 Because I spend a lot of time in airports, I meet a lot of pilots. I also have a couple of pilot friends. So I know a lot about pilots' lives. The most interesting people are long-haul pilots: pilots who fly very long distances (6+ hours!). They need a lot of training. First, they go to flight school for 1.5 to 2 years. After that, they spend a few years working as a first officer. Then, to become a long-haul pilot, they need to fly for 5,000+ hours. In total, that takes at least six years. Long-haul pilots cannot fly more than 100 hours per month, and they normally fly much less.

Pilots in an airplane's cockpit

2. First, long-haul pilots go _____ .

The Flight Routine

3 Long-haul pilots always get to the airport early and immediately go through security, just like you and me. But while you shop or have something to eat, pilots meet with their crew—the other pilots and the flight attendants. Then it's time for departure. This is the really busy part of the flight. But after takeoff, the work is easier: The pilots put on the autopilot and check that everything is safe and going well. Finally, it's time to land the plane. Before the landing, they spend time planning for it. Planning and doing the landing usually takes an hour. After they land, they go home or to a hotel, where they sometimes stay for a week without working.

3. After arriving at the airport before a flight, pilots immediately _____
_____ .

The Good and the Bad

4 There are definitely a lot of good things about becoming a long-haul pilot: The pay is good, and you can travel all around the world. But there's the jet lag. Some pilots have good routines for jet lag: They exercise immediately after they land and then take a short nap. These pilots may not have much jet lag, but others feel the pain of always traveling. Also, pilots with families spend a lot of time away from home. So, for me, I think I'll keep my job as a writer.

4. To help with jet lag, some pilots _____ .

C. Look at your predictions again. Were they correct?

🔵 Go to **MyEnglishLab** to reread the text.

READ AGAIN

A. Read the text again. Then read the statements below. Circle *T* (true) or *F* (false).

T / F   1. A flight from New York to Rome is less than seven hours.

T / F   2. Long-haul flights are 6+ hours long.

T / F   3. Flight school takes 18 to 24 months to finish.

T / F   4. Long-haul pilots need 5,000+ flight hours.

T / F   5. Long-haul pilots fly for 100+ hours per month.

T / F   6. It usually takes an hour for a pilot to plan and do a landing.

B. Read the steps of a pilot's routine. Put them in the correct order (1–6).

_____ meet with other pilots and flight attendants   _____ turn on autopilot

_____ go home or to a hotel   _1_ go through security

_____ plan for landing and land the airplane   _____ do the takeoff

C. Work with a partner. Compare your answers in Parts A and B. Correct the false statements in Part A.

D. Read the questions. Discuss them with a partner or in a small group.

1. What are good things about the job of a long-haul pilot? What are the bad things?

2. It takes a long time to become a long-haul pilot. Do you think it's worth it? That is, is it a good idea to spend a lot of time training and preparing for the job? Why or why not?

3. Is it easy to understand numbers when you read? Why or why not? Is it easy to understand routines when you read? Why or why not?

VOCABULARY REVIEW

Complete the sentences with the words from the box.

departure	immediately	pay	flights	lands	training

1. You can get your bags after the plane _____ .

2. The _____ for the job isn't good, but I get a lot of vacation time!

3. Teachers get years of _____ so they can learn how to teach well.

4. There is a list of _____ times on that screen. You can find out when your plane leaves.

5. Every day, there are many _____ between London and Dubai.

6. I'm always so tired that I fall asleep _____ after I get in bed.

THINK VISUALLY

Read the questions. Discuss them with a partner or in a small group.

1. The bar chart shows the average amount of sleep that people who do these six jobs get: airline pilots, athletes, doctors, lawyers, police officers, and teachers. Who gets the most sleep? Who gets the least sleep? Guess how to label the bars in the chart. Write the jobs on the lines.

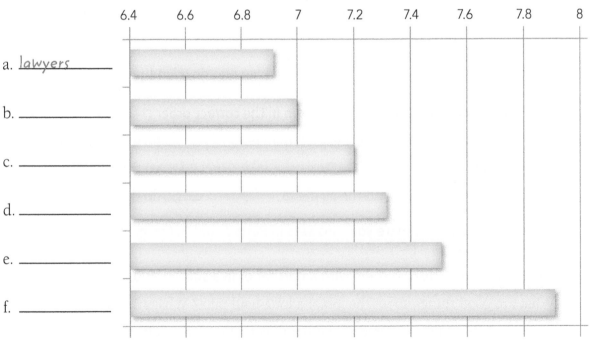

Average Amount of Sleep for People in Different Jobs (in Hours)

a. lawyers

b. _____

c. _____

d. _____

e. _____

f. _____

2. Look at the answer key on page 169. Were your guesses correct? Are any of the answers surprising? Why or why not?

GRAMMAR

USING ADVERBS OF FREQUENCY AND *EVERY*

Circle the correct answers.

1. Megan **never / always / usually** falls asleep before 9 P.M. She stays up late every night.

2. **Usually / Often / Sometimes** Jan goes for a walk after work—it's part of her routine. But she's really busy today, so she can't.

3. Pietro **is / sleeps / wakes up** never late.

4. I **usually / sometimes / always** eat breakfast. I never leave my house in the morning without eating.

5. Pilots **always / usually / sometimes** spend a few years in training before they start working at an airline company.

6. I exercise every day. How **never / often / sometimes** do you exercise?

ASSIGNMENT

Write a paragraph about another student's routine.

PREPARE TO WRITE

A. Work with a partner. Interview your partner to find out about his or her routine. Write the answers in the spaces provided.

1. What time do you usually wake up? _____

2. Do you eat breakfast? What do you usually eat? What time do you usually eat?

   _____

   _____

3. What time do you go to school / work? _____

4. What do you do first at school / work? _____

5. Do you eat lunch? What do you usually eat? What time do you usually eat?

   _____

   _____

6. What do you do after school / work? _____

   _____

7. How often do you exercise or play sports? How many hours?

   _____

8. What time do you eat dinner? _____

9. What time do you go to sleep? _____

10. How many hours do you sleep? _____

11. What special or unusual daily / weekly routines do you have? Describe one of them.

    _____

    _____

B. Look at your partner's answers in Part A. Will you describe a daily routine or a routine for just one day a week (for example, something your partner does every Saturday)? Do not include everything. Focus on the interesting parts of a routine. Plan your writing in the space below. See the example.

Tuesday after-school routine
1. 3:30 she finishes class, gets coffee
2. 4:00–6:00 she has band practice
3. 6:00 she goes to dinner with friends from band

1.
2.
3.
4.
5.
6.
7.
8.

WRITE

Write a paragraph about your partner's routine. Begin with a sentence to introduce your topic. Here are some examples:

Franco has a busy morning routine.

Jin has fun on Saturdays.

Use time signal words like *before* and *then* to connect the ideas between sentences. Give your paragraph a title.

PROOFREAD AND EDIT

A. Proofread your paragraph.

- Do you have an introductory sentence and a title?

- Do you use words that show order (for example, *before*, *then*, and *after*)?

- Do you use adverbs of frequency and *every* correctly?

- Are there any spelling mistakes?

B. Work with your partner. Share your paragraphs. Answer the questions in the Peer Review Form. Share feedback. Then edit your paragraph.

Peer Review Form	Yes	No
1. Does your partner write about your routine clearly and correctly?	☐	☐
2. Does your partner focus on one topic in his or her writing?	☐	☐
3. Does your partner use signal words that show order (for example, *before*, *then*, and *after*)?	☐	☐
4. Are the sentences in the form of a paragraph?	☐	☐
5. Are there any spelling mistakes? If there are, circle them.	☐	☐

Answer Key for Think Visually, page 166

b. doctors, c. police officers, d. teachers, e. airline pilots, f. athletes

○ Go to **MyEnglishLab** to complete grammar and vocabulary practices.

DEVELOP SOFT SKILLS

MAKING HEALTHY CHOICES

The work you do for your college courses will keep you busy most of the time. It's also important to find time to take care of yourself—both your mind and your body. Getting enough sleep, eating well, hanging out with friends, and exercising are all important for staying healthy. It's a good idea to make exercising part of your routine.

A. Read the words and definitions. You will see these words in the text.

> ### Glossary
>
> athlete: a person who does sports
> compete: try to win in a sports event
> flexible: able to move and bend easily
> on your own: alone, without anyone's help
> work out: do exercise to make your body fit and strong

B. Read the text.

Making Exercise Part of Your Routine

1   As a college student, you probably sit when you are in class, sit when you study, sit in the dining hall, and sit at your computer. That is a lot of sitting! The good news is, there are a lot of fun ways to make exercising part of your routine.

Playing Team and Individual Sports

2   Most colleges and universities have team sports, like basketball and soccer. You can play on a team organized by the school and compete against other school teams, or you can organize a team for fun with your friends.

3   Most schools also have individual sports, like tennis and swimming. The athletes who do these sports practice with their teams but compete alone. Playing a college sport can be both hard work—practicing a few times a week—and great fun.

Working Out on Your Own

4   Another possibility is working out on your own. For example, maybe your school has a pool where you can swim or a gym where you can run on a treadmill. Or maybe your school or community has classes for yoga, dance, or martial arts (like karate or taekwondo). All of these can help make you stronger and more flexible. Another good thing about working out on your own: You can do it on your own time.

Running on a treadmill

Moving Anytime, Anywhere

5 Maybe your school doesn't have a pool. Or maybe you don't have time for a class. Or maybe the idea of "exercise" just isn't your thing. It's OK! Just moving can help you stay healthy. For example, walking is very good for you. Climbing stairs is good, too. What about dancing? It's easy: Just turn on some music you like and move. The best thing about these activities? You can do them anytime, anywhere.

C. Read the statements. Circle *T* (true) or *F* (false). Correct the false statements.

T / F   1. Exercise is a way to stay healthy.

T / F   2. You need to play sports to get enough exercise.

T / F   3. Basketball and soccer are examples of individual sports.

T / F   4. Doing yoga and taking martial arts classes are ways to work out.

T / F   5. You need to be on a team or in a class if you want to work out.

T / F   6. Walking, dancing, and stretching are forms of exercise.

D. The text gives examples of ways to exercise. Write them in the chart. With a partner, add your ideas. Underline the activities you like. Circle the ones you want to try.

Team sports	
Individual sports	
Classes you can take	
Other ways to exercise on your own	

E. Answer the questions. Proofread and edit your sentences. Then share them with a partner.

1. What do you do for exercise?

   _____

   _____

2. How often do you exercise?

   _____

   _____

3. What new way to exercise would you like to try?

   _____

   _____

Dancing is great exercise.

WHAT DID YOU LEARN?

Check (✓) the skills and vocabulary you learned. Circle the things you need to practice.

SKILLS

☐ I can understand numbers in a text.

☐ I can connect ideas between sentences.

☐ I can use adverbs of frequency and *every*.

☐ I can use vocabulary for daily activities.

☐ I can make healthy choices.

VOCABULARY

☐ accident

☐ adult

☐ average

☐ calories

☐ competition

☐ dangerous

☐ departure

☐ do taekwondo

☐ do yoga

☐ enough

☐ fall asleep

☐ flight

☐ go running

☐ go swimming

☐ gym

☐ hang out

☐ immediately

☐ land

☐ nap

☐ pay

☐ play baseball

☐ play basketball

☐ play the piano

☐ play soccer

☐ play video games

☐ training

☐ wake up

☐ while

① Go to **MyEnglishLab** to complete a self-assessment.

| Chapter 8 | # The Stories We Dream |

CHAPTER PROFILE

Dreams tell us stories. Our sleeping brains fill our minds with images and feelings that seem real. Dreams can take us on adventures.

This chapter is about dreams and the stories they tell. You will learn about dreams, and through dreams, you will understand stories better.

You will read about

• what dreams are and why we have dreams.

• the life of a famous psychologist who studied dreams.

• dreams and their interpretations.

You will write about your personal history and a dream that you had.

OUTCOMES

• Understand narratives
• Write personal stories
• Use the simple past
• Understand basic suffixes
• Use flashcards to learn new vocabulary

For more about **PSYCHOLOGY**, see Chapter 7. See also |OC| **PSYCHOLOGY**, Chapters 7 and 8.

GETTING STARTED

Read the questions. Discuss them with a partner or in a small group.

1. Look at the picture to the right. What is the woman doing?

2. Dreams are like stories in our sleep. Do your dreams tell stories about you? Explain.

⬆ Go to **MyEnglishLab** to complete a self-assessment.

READ

SKILL: UNDERSTANDING NARRATIVES

Narratives are stories. In English, narratives have a simple structure (organization of parts). They have three main parts: a **beginning**, a **middle**, and an **ending**.

- The beginning introduces the main **characters** (the people in the story) and the **setting** (the place of the story). (Sometimes characters are introduced later and settings change.)
- In the middle, we learn about the story's **plot** (the main events) and the **conflict** (a problem or fight) for the characters.
- The ending of the story includes the last big event of the story and its **results** (what happens after).

Knowing the different parts of a story can help you to understand narratives.

A. Read the story. Notice its beginning, middle, and ending.

Golden Dreams (a story from *The Arabian Nights*)

Muhammad Ali Mosque, Cairo

1 Once upon a time, there was a man named Farid. He lived in Baghdad. Farid had a lot of money problems. One night, he had a dream. In the dream, a voice told him to go to Cairo. There, the voice said, Farid would find a lot of money. So Farid went to Cairo.

2 But after arriving in Cairo, the police arrested Farid because they thought he stole from a mosque. He was upset and decided to tell the police about his dream. After hearing about the dream, one police officer said that he had the same dream. But in the police officer's dream, the money was near Farid's house.

3 The police sent Farid back to Baghdad. When Farid got there, he looked for the money—and found it! He shared the money with his friends and family, and he told people to pay attention to their dreams.

CULTURE NOTE

The phrase *once upon a time*, meaning "long, long ago," is the usual way to begin a children's fairy tale or another traditional story.

B. Look at the timeline. It shows the order of events in "Golden Dreams."

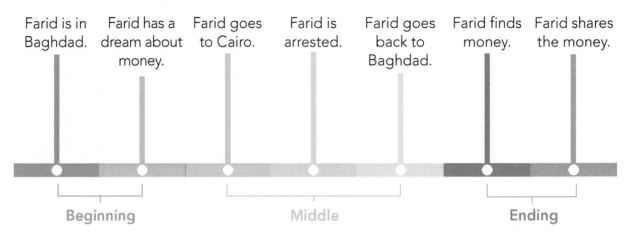

| Farid is in Baghdad. | Farid has a dream about money. | Farid goes to Cairo. | Farid is arrested. | Farid goes back to Baghdad. | Farid finds money. | Farid shares the money. |

Beginning   Middle   Ending

All texts in English—stories, movies, and academic writing—are based on this basic narrative structure. Understand it well and you will be on your way to understanding more difficult texts.

THE STRUCTURE OF A BASIC NARRATIVE		
Part of Story	**Key Points**	**Example from "Golden Dreams"**
Beginning	Character(s)	Farid
	Setting	Baghdad, Cairo
	First event	Farid dreams about hearing a voice.
Middle	Main event(s) of the plot	Farid travels to Cairo.
	Conflict	Farid is arrested.
Ending	Last event	Farid finds money.
	Results	Farid shares the money and tells people to pay attention to their dreams.

CULTURE NOTE

The beginning of a story often gives the **background**, information about the characters and setting that is important for the story's plot.

REMEMBER

Match the parts of the sentences.

_____ 1. In the beginning of a story, we learn about …

_____ 2. In the middle, we learn about …

_____ 3. In the ending, we learn about …

a. the main event and conflict.

b. the last big event and its results.

c. the characters and setting.

VOCABULARY PREVIEW

A. Read the sentences. Look at the boldfaced words and phrases. Do you know what they mean? Share your ideas with a partner.

1. We did many things today, but after the long day, we are **back at** home now.

2. When you think, you are using your **brain**!

3. Terry has a **busy** day today. He has many meetings and a lot of work.

4. My friend loves computers. She **created** an app to help people remember their dreams.

5. The rabbit lives in a **hole** in the ground.

6. Eating food and drinking water are **necessary** for life.

7. In dreams, a horse can **represent** power and strength or a person who is strong and powerful.

8. People, especially children, often have **strange** dreams about talking animals or unknown places.

9. There was a sound at my front door. **Suddenly**, my dog jumped up and ran to the door.

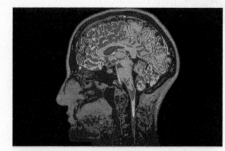

B. Write the boldfaced words and phrases from Part A next to their definitions.

_____ 1. the part of your body that is inside your head

_____ 2. not normal, difficult to understand

_____ 3. describing something that you need or must do

_____ 4. used when something happens quickly, often by surprise

_____ 5. doing many things

_____ 6. made something

_____ 7. describes returning to a place

_____ 8. a space with nothing in it

_____ 9. be a symbol of

➊ Go to **MyEnglishLab** to complete a vocabulary practice.

Look at the title and pictures. Which questions will the text answer? Check (✓) your ideas.

☐ Do dreams tell stories?

☐ Does everyone dream?

☐ Do animals dream?

☐ Why do we have dreams?

☐ When do we have dreams?

☐ Is there anything we don't know about dreams?

READ

A. Read the text. Complete the sentences after each section.

Dreams Tell Stories

1 Alice, a young girl, is sitting beside a river on a beautiful summer day. Suddenly, a white rabbit runs by. But there's something strange about the rabbit: He's wearing clothes and talking. He looks at his watch and says, "Oh dear! I'm late!" Alice follows him to a hole in the ground and jumps in after him. She starts to fall. She falls for a very long time. Finally, she lands in a magical world. It's a world with talking animals. The animals have parties! There's also a queen who wants to kill Alice. But then, suddenly, Alice wakes up. She's back at the river, and she realizes that it was all a dream. This dream is the story of *Alice's Adventures in Wonderland*.

The White Rabbit from
Alice's Adventures in Wonderland

1. The setting of the story is _____ .

    a. Alice, many talking animals, and a queen

    b. a place near a river and a magical world with talking animals

2. The conflict in *Alice's Adventures in Wonderland* is with _____ .

    a. the queen

    b. the animals

3. The ending of the story is _____.

   a. Alice waking up at the river

   b. Alice jumping into the rabbit hole

4. *Alice's Adventures in Wonderland* is a story about _____.

   a. a dream

   b. sleeping

2 Dreams are stories that our brain creates while we sleep. Most dreams happen when the brain is very busy—a time during sleep called REM sleep. (*REM* is short for rapid eye movement). Everyone dreams, but not everyone remembers his or her dreams.

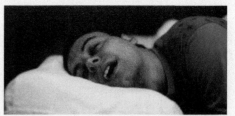

Is he dreaming?

5. REM sleep is the time during sleep when _____.

   a. most dreams happen

   b. the brain rests quietly

3 So why do we dream? In ancient Greece, many people believed dreams were messages from the gods (powerful beings). But in India, many people thought dreams represented our desires (things we want). The famous psychologist (a person who works in psychology) Dr. Sigmund Freud agreed. Today, scientists believe that dreaming is necessary for learning, remembering, and having good mental health.

A statue of a Greek god

4 The truth is that we don't fully understand dreams. But we do know that they often tell us strange stories about ourselves and the world around us.

6. Scientists understand _____ about dreams.

   a. everything

   b. some things

CULTURE NOTE

Mental health is the condition of your mind, feelings, and thoughts.

B. Look at your predictions again. Were they correct?

🔊 **Go to MyEnglishLab to reread the text.**

READ AGAIN

A. Read Paragraph 1 again. Then complete the timeline.

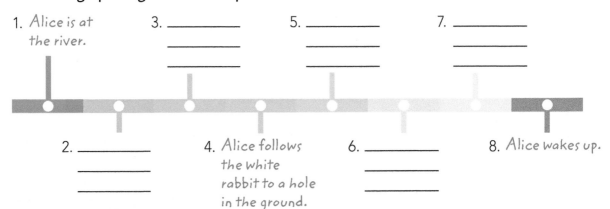

1. *Alice is at the river.*

3. _____ _____ _____

5. _____ _____ _____

7. _____ _____ _____

2. _____ _____ _____

4. *Alice follows the white rabbit to a hole in the ground.*

6. _____ _____ _____

8. *Alice wakes up.*

B. Read the rest of the text again. Then read the statements below. Circle *T* (true) or *F* (false).

T / F   1. Dreams are stories that our brain creates.

T / F   2. Dreams usually happen during REM sleep.

T / F   3. REM sleep happens when the brain is not very active.

T / F   4. In India, many people thought that dreams were messages.

T / F   5. Dr. Sigmund Freud thought that dreams represented desires.

T / F   6. Dreams are important for learning and remembering things.

C. Work with a partner. Compare your answers in Parts A and B. Correct the false statements in Part B.

D. Read the questions. Discuss them with a partner.

1. *Alice's Adventures in Wonderland* is a story about a dream. Do you know of any other stories (video games, books, or movies) that are about dreams? What are they?

2. Do you dream often? Do you remember your dreams? Explain.

3. Is it easy to understand narratives? Why? What are the main parts of narratives?

VOCABULARY REVIEW

Complete the sentences with the words and phrases from the box.

back at	busy	hole	represent	suddenly
brain	created	necessary	strange	

1. There's a big _____ in the floor. Someone will get hurt. We need to fix it!

2. I had a _____ dream last night. There were a lot of animals, and all of them could understand me.

3. The doctor is _____. She can't meet with you right now.

4. In dreams, dangerous situations can _____ problems in your life.

5. The _____ is the center of our thoughts and feelings. It's the most important part of our body.

6. It's _____ for children to get a lot of sleep. It's important for their health and for doing well at school.

7. We started in Japan and then traveled to Korea and China. Now we are _____ our hotel in Japan and will stay here for one more week.

8. Andrea told her boss she hated her job. _____, she woke up. She had been dreaming.

9. A famous architect _____ the design for this building.

○ Go to **MyEnglishLab** to read another text.

WRITE

SKILL: WRITING PERSONAL STORIES

As you read in "Dreams Tell Stories," dreams are stories that the brain creates when we sleep. If we remember a dream, we talk about it using a narrative structure: a beginning, a middle, and an ending.

In this section, we will look at how to write one kind of **personal story**: a personal history, or true story about your past experiences.

Before you write a personal history, first use a timeline to plan your writing. Make notes about important events. Plan for the beginning, middle, and ending of your story. Study the example below.

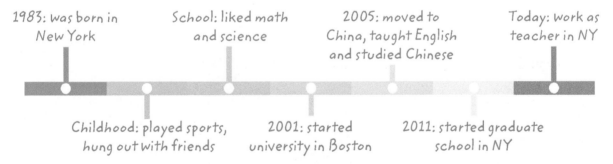

1983: was born in New York

School: liked math and science

2005: moved to China, taught English and studied Chinese

Today: work as teacher in NY

Childhood: played sports, hung out with friends

2001: started university in Boston

2011: started graduate school in NY

Next, write your story in the form of a paragraph. Follow these steps:

1. Introduce the main character (you). This is the beginning of your personal history.

2. Write about some big events in your life. Include information about your childhood (the time when you were a child) and big changes. This is the middle of your story.

3. Connect the events in order. Use **time markers** (for example, *in 2015*, *three years ago*). Use **time signal words** (for example, *then* and *after*).

4. Write a concluding sentence about your situation today. This is the ending of your story.

Look at this example of a personal history. It is based on the timeline on page 181. It has a beginning, a middle, and an ending.

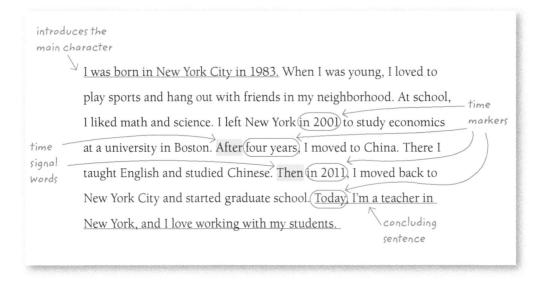

introduces the main character

I was born in New York City in 1983. When I was young, I loved to play sports and hang out with friends in my neighborhood. At school, I liked math and science. I left New York in 2001 to study economics at a university in Boston. After four years, I moved to China. There I taught English and studied Chinese. Then in 2011, I moved back to New York City and started graduate school. Today, I'm a teacher in New York, and I love working with my students.

time markers

time signal words

concluding sentence

To become a good writer, you must learn how to tell a story. Writing stories will help you to become a good academic writer, too.

TIP

When planning to write a story or personal narrative, use a timeline. Timelines can help you to see the order of the events in a story.

REMEMBER

Complete the sentences.

1. Focus on _____ in your narrative.

2. Use _____ to show when events happen.

3. Use _____ to connect sentences in order.

Grammar for Writing Using the simple past

When we tell stories, especially about our experiences, we use verbs in the **simple past**. We use them to talk about actions and events that started and finished in the past:

I **went** to the store last night. (I am not at the store now.)

Jeremy **studied** in France a few years ago. (Jeremy is not studying in France now.)

We often use time markers with the simple past. These are some common time markers:

- *yesterday*
- *last (night / week / year)*
- *(two / five / ten) years ago*
- *in (2009)*

Use the simple past in your writing to tell stories about events that happened in the past.

THE SIMPLE PAST TENSE			
	Rules	**Examples**	**Example Sentences**
Regular verbs	Add: -ed -d -ied	play play**ed** move move**d** study stud**ied**	I **played** basketball yesterday. Kara **moved** to Dubai five years ago. My brother **studied** many things in college.
Irregular verbs	Each verb has a different form.	go **went** see **saw** teach **taught**	My mother **went** to Europe last year. I **saw** a good movie last night. She **taught** Chinese for 15 years.
Negative verbs	Use *did not* + base form of verb	**did not (didn't) play** **did not (didn't) go**	Lauren **did not play** basketball yesterday. Kelsey **didn't go** to the store.
The verb *be*	Two forms: Negatives:	I / he / she / it **was** you / we / they **were** I / he / she / it **was not (wasn't)** you / we / they **were not (weren't)**	It **was** very cold yesterday. They **were** very busy last week. Fatima **was not** in class yesterday. You **weren't** happy about your test scores.

More Irregular Verbs							
become	**became**	find	**found**	leave	**left**	take	**took**
begin	**began**	get	**got**	make	**made**	tell	**told**
buy	**bought**	give	**gave**	meet	**met**	think	**thought**
come	**came**	have	**had**	read	**read**	wake up	**woke up**
fall	**fell**	hear	**heard**	say	**said**	write	**wrote**
feel	**felt**	know	**knew**	sleep	**slept**		

Complete the sentence.

We use the simple past to talk about actions and events that _____ and _____ in the past.

A. Complete the sentences with the verbs. Use the correct simple past form.

1. Taka _____ (**go**) to the movies yesterday.

2. Beth _____ (**listen**) to music for hours last night.

3. Wenjing _____ (**give**) her parents a nice gift.

4. Our teacher _____ (**tell**) us to study hard for the final exam.

5. I looked for my keys in my room, but I _____ (**not, find**) them.

6. The author _____ (**write**) his first book in 1993.

7. Nancy _____ (**not, like**) her new shoes, so she returned them for a refund.

8. My sister _____ (**teach**) me how to ride a bike.

B. Circle the correct form of the verb to complete each sentence.

1. I **see / saw** a movie about dreams last weekend.

2. Kim **exercises / exercised** at the gym last night.

3. Mike loves his grandmother. He **visits / visited** her every weekend.

4. Amy and Sara **don't / didn't** come to the party yesterday.

5. We **move / moved** to London three years ago.

6. I **feel / felt** really tired, so I'll take a nap.

7. Taiki didn't **play / played** soccer when he was a child.

8. Alejandro **starts / started** studying English in 2017.

C. Read the paragraph. Find and correct the seven mistakes with verbs.

When I am young, I like to read. I read books about lots of topics: psychology, sports, architecture—everything. Then, when I started college in 2003, I begin writing short stories. I write a lot during that time. I continue writing after graduating. In 2016, I finish my first book. It was a hit! Millions of people buy it in 2017 alone. Now I'm working on another book, and I still love to read.

○ Go to **MyEnglishLab** for more grammar practice.

WRITE ABOUT YOUR PERSONAL HISTORY

STEP 1: READ TO WRITE

A. Read the words and definitions. You will see these words in the text.

> ### Glossary
>
> **current:** happening now, at the present time
>
> **experience:** something that you do, something that happens to you
>
> **live on:** continue to be
>
> **memory:** something that you remember from the past
>
> **mind:** a person's thoughts and feelings
>
> **patient:** a person with health problems that gets help from doctors
>
> **solve:** find an answer to a problem
>
> **stay with:** always be in a person's mind

B. Read the text. Complete the task after each section.

The Life of Sigmund Freud

Sigmund Freud

1 Sigmund Freud was an Austrian neurologist (a doctor that studies the brain and the rest of the nervous system). He is one of the most important people in psychology and is best known for his work on dream interpretation (the way we find meaning in dreams) and mental health. This is his story.

2 Freud was born in 1856 in Freiberg, Austria (now part of the Czech Republic). As a child, he learned to read in eight different languages, including French, English, and Greek. At 17, he began university in Vienna. By the age of 25, he was a medical doctor. He focused on the human brain, its structure, and how it worked.

> 1. Underline the sentence in Paragraph 2 that introduces the story of Dr. Freud's life. Circle the time markers in Paragraph 2.

3 Freud became interested in people's mental health problems. He believed that people had these problems because they repressed—did not think about—bad experiences from their past. But the bad experiences stayed with them in a part of the mind called the *unconscious*. Dreams, Freud thought, were stories told by the unconscious about past experiences—good and bad.

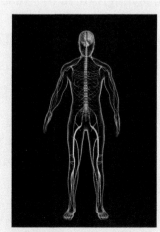

The nervous system

2. Freud thought that people's mental health problems _____ .

    a. were not interesting

    b. came from their past experiences

    c. came from bad experiences in their daily routines

4 Studying dreams helped people solve their problems, Freud believed. He felt that understanding the past was an important step in fixing the future. So he created psychoanalysis: the process of talking about dreams and desires. With a doctor, patients remember their past. These memories help patients to understand their current problems.

5 Freud died in 1939, but his work lives on. Today, psychoanalysis is still popular. And psychologists and other scientists see Freud as one of the most important thinkers of the 20th century.

3. Underline the concluding sentences about Dr. Freud.

C. Read the events in Dr. Freud's life. Number them in the correct order (1–7).

_____ He died.

_____ He learned to read in many languages.

_____ He created psychoanalysis.

__1__ Sigmund Freud was born.

_____ He started university.

_____ He became interested in mental health.

_____ He became a doctor.

❖ Go to **MyEnglishLab** to reread the text.

STEP 2: PREPARE TO WRITE

A. Read the questions. Discuss them with a partner or in a small group.

1. When were you born? Do you have brothers and sisters? When were they born?

2. When you were young, what activities did you like to do—for example, did you play sports, study school subjects, or hang out with friends? Did you go to different schools or universities? When did you start them? Did you make new friends?

3. In the past, did you travel anywhere? Did you ever move to a new place?

4. Did you meet a person who became important in your life? Who was the person?

5. Did you learn a new skill that was or is important to you?

B. Make a timeline of the events in your life. Use years to show when the events happened.

I was born.

STEP 3: WRITE

Write a paragraph of five or more sentences about your personal history. Be sure to focus on you and the big events in your life. Use time markers and time signal words. End with a concluding sentence about your current situation. Give your paragraph a title.

_____

_____

_____

_____

_____

STEP 4: PROOFREAD AND EDIT

A. Proofread your paragraph.

- Do you write about the big events of your life?

- Do you have a concluding sentence to tell about your current situation?

- Do your sentences form a paragraph?

- Do you use time markers and time signal words?

- Do you use the simple past correctly?

- Are there any spelling mistakes?

B. Work with your partner. Share your paragraphs. Answer the questions in the Peer Review Form. Share feedback. Then edit your paragraph.

Peer Review Form	Yes	No
1. Does your partner focus on the big events in his or her life?	☐	☐
2. Does your partner include a concluding sentence to tell about his or her current situation?	☐	☐
3. Does your partner use time markers and time signal words correctly?	☐	☐
4. Does your partner use the simple past correctly?	☐	☐
5. Are there any spelling mistakes? If there are, circle them.	☐	☐

C. Work with a partner. Answer the questions.

1. When you write about your personal history, what events should you write about?

2. Is it easy to write a personal narrative? Is it interesting to read about your partner's personal history? Explain.

BUILDING VOCABULARY

UNDERSTANDING BASIC SUFFIXES

To make your writing more interesting, use many different words. One way to grow your vocabulary is to learn and add **suffixes** to the base forms of verbs. A suffix is a letter, or letters, added to the end of a word to form a new word.

Study the chart.

Base Word (verb)	Suffix		New Word (noun)	Meaning of Noun with Suffix
read write teach fry	-er / -r	+	reader writer teacher fryer	a person or device that does the action
mean end feel	-ing	=	meaning ending feeling	a thing or idea

GRAMMAR NOTE

For most verbs that end in consonant + vowel (*a, e, i, o, u, y*) + consonant, like the *-wim* in *swim*, we double the final consonant before adding *-er*, as in the noun *swimmer*.

GRAMMAR NOTE

The ending *-ing* is also used for present progressive verbs: *She is swimming in the pool.*

A. Look at the pictures. Complete the chart with the verb or noun form of each word.

	Verb	Noun		Verb	Noun
1.	_____	 runner	5.	print	 _____
2.	climb	 _____	6.	begin	 _____
3.	_____	 driver	7.	_____	 ending
4.	travel	 _____	8.	meet	 _____

B. Write the words from the box next to their definitions.

| beginner | hacker | ~~painting~~ | train |
| ending | meeting | printer | |

painting   1. a piece of art

_____ 2. a device that puts words on paper

_____ 3. a time and place where people come together

_____ 4. a person who steals things using a computer

_____ 5. teach someone a skill for a job

_____ 6. a person who is new at learning or playing something

_____ 7. the final part of a story

C. Circle the correct word to complete each sentence.

1. The **print / printer** is broken again! Can somebody fix it?

2. I don't understand the **mean / meaning** of this word.

3. The **climb / climber** fell and hurt his leg.

4. There is an introductory English course for **begins / beginners** at my school.

5. Kay and Drew often **run / runner** together in the morning and go to the gym at night.

6. I'm late. Can you **drive / driver** me to school today?

⏴ Go to **MyEnglishLab** to complete a vocabulary practice.

APPLY YOUR SKILLS

In this chapter, you read about how dreams tell us stories about ourselves. You also learned about the life of Dr. Sigmund Freud and his ideas about dreams. You wrote about your life—your personal history. In Apply Your Skills, you will read about dreams and their interpretations (the meanings we find in dreams). You will then write about one of your dreams.

VOCABULARY PREVIEW

A. Read the sentences. Look at the boldfaced words and phrases. Do you know what they mean? Share your ideas with a partner.

1. I'm **afraid** of many animals—especially birds! I don't want to go near them.

2. Don't **avoid** your problems. Try to solve them right away.

3. A rat **bit** Tina. Now she has to go to the hospital.

4. In my dream, a big rabbit **chased** me. So I ran into my house.

5. I have a **fear** of cats. I get really upset when I see them.

6. There are thousands of different animals in the **jungle**.

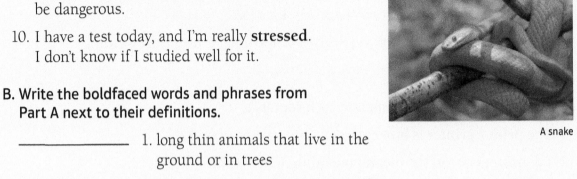

A jungle

7. Tracy hates frogs. She **ran away** from the lake when she saw one.

8. In dreams, you can fly or meet talking animals, but that doesn't happen in **real life**.

9. **Snakes** are beautiful animals, but they can be dangerous.

10. I have a test today, and I'm really **stressed**. I don't know if I studied well for it.

A snake

B. Write the boldfaced words and phrases from Part A next to their definitions.

_____ 1. long thin animals that live in the ground or in trees

_____ 2. left quickly to get far from something

_____ 3. events and experiences in the world, not events in stories

_____ 4. feeling that something bad will happen to you, frightened (of something)

_____ 5. used its teeth to eat something or hurt someone

_____ 6. try not to do something

_____ 7. feeling worried

_____ 8. a hot place where there are many trees and other plants close together

_____ 9. a feeling of being afraid that something bad will happen to you

_____ 10. followed someone, usually by running after them

🔊 Go to **MyEnglishLab** to complete a vocabulary practice.

PREDICT

Look at subject of the emails: *a terrible dream*. What information do you think you will find in the emails? Write two predictions.

1. I will find information about _____ .

2. I will find information about _____ .

READ

A. Read the text. Answer the question after each section.

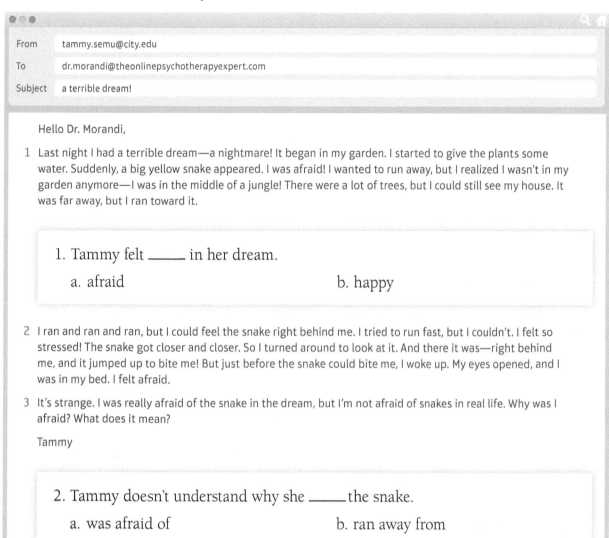

From tammy.semu@city.edu

To dr.morandi@theonlinepsychotherapyexpert.com

Subject a terrible dream!

Hello Dr. Morandi,

1 Last night I had a terrible dream—a nightmare! It began in my garden. I started to give the plants some water. Suddenly, a big yellow snake appeared. I was afraid! I wanted to run away, but I realized I wasn't in my garden anymore—I was in the middle of a jungle! There were a lot of trees, but I could still see my house. It was far away, but I ran toward it.

> **1. Tammy felt _____ in her dream.**
>
> a. afraid   b. happy

2 I ran and ran and ran, but I could feel the snake right behind me. I tried to run fast, but I couldn't. I felt so stressed! The snake got closer and closer. So I turned around to look at it. And there it was—right behind me, and it jumped up to bite me! But just before the snake could bite me, I woke up. My eyes opened, and I was in my bed. I felt afraid.

3 It's strange. I was really afraid of the snake in the dream, but I'm not afraid of snakes in real life. Why was I afraid? What does it mean?

Tammy

> **2. Tammy doesn't understand why she _____ the snake.**
>
> a. was afraid of   b. ran away from

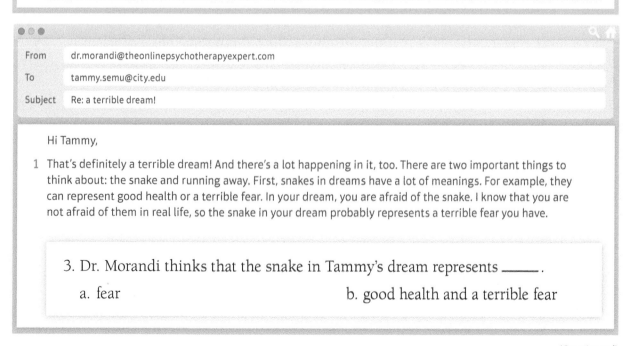

From dr.morandi@theonlinepsychotherapyexpert.com

To tammy.semu@city.edu

Subject Re: a terrible dream!

Hi Tammy,

1 That's definitely a terrible dream! And there's a lot happening in it, too. There are two important things to think about: the snake and running away. First, snakes in dreams have a lot of meanings. For example, they can represent good health or a terrible fear. In your dream, you are afraid of the snake. I know that you are not afraid of them in real life, so the snake in your dream probably represents a terrible fear you have.

> **3. Dr. Morandi thinks that the snake in Tammy's dream represents _____ .**
>
> a. fear   b. good health and a terrible fear

(Continued)

2 Also, the snake chased you in the dream, and you *ran away* from it. You were afraid. This means that you are avoiding—running away from—a problem, or maybe a fear. Are you avoiding something in real life? Is it something you're afraid of? Your dream is telling you to solve this problem. Think about it. And watch out for snakes if you're in the garden this weekend!

Best,

Dr. Morandi

4. Dr. Morandi thinks that Tammy _____ in real life.

   a. is afraid of snakes   b. has a problem

B. Look at your predictions again. Were they correct?

🔾 Go to **MyEnglishLab** to reread the text.

READ AGAIN

A. Read the text again. Then read the statements below. Circle *T* (true) or *F* (false).

T / F   1. Dr. Morandi is an online psychotherapy expert.

T / F   2. Tammy first saw the snake in the jungle.

T / F   3. Tammy didn't see her house in the jungle.

T / F   4. The snake bit Tammy before she woke up.

T / F   5. Tammy is not afraid of snakes in real life.

T / F   6. Dr. Morandi says that snakes represent good things and bad things.

T / F   7. Dr. Morandi thinks that the dream is telling Tammy she has a problem.

B. Work with a partner. Compare your answers in Part A. Correct the false statements.

C. Read the questions. Discuss them with a partner or in a small group.

1. Do you have dreams that are similar to Tammy's? That is, do you have dreams of someone or something chasing you? Who or what chases you? Where are you? Where do you run to?

2. Dr. Morandi says that the snake represents a problem or a fear. Do you agree? If not, what do you think the snake represents? What do snakes represent in your culture?

3. What are the three parts of a narrative? Can you understand a story without understanding one of these parts? Explain.

VOCABULARY REVIEW

Complete the sentences with the words and phrases from the box.

afraid	bit	fear	ran away	snakes
avoids	chased	jungle	real life	stressed

1. _____ don't have legs, but they can move along the ground very fast.

2. Jermaine has a _____ of flying. He never travels anywhere by airplane.

3. My five-year-old brother is _____ of rabbits. He cries when he sees them.

4. In my dream, I was a criminal. The police _____ me all around the world, but they couldn't catch me.

5. Emma is always so _____. Maybe it's because she works so much.

6. Yelina _____ eating sweet foods, like candy and cake. She tries to eat healthy food instead.

7. Liz lives and works in a _____ in South America. She studies the trees there.

8. There were a few cats in my yard yesterday. I went outside to play with them, but they _____.

9. I didn't eat all day yesterday. So when I finally _____ into my sandwich last night, it tasted so good.

10. Dreams can sometimes be similar to _____, but they are often very different.

THINK VISUALLY

Look at the pictures and discuss the questions with a partner or in a small group.

A

B

C

D

1. What's happening in each picture? Describe the people and situations.

2. In the Apply Your Skills reading, Dr. Morandi says that running away means that Tammy is avoiding her problems or fears. Look again at the pictures. As dreams, what could the pictures mean?

GRAMMAR

USING THE SIMPLE PAST

Complete the sentences. Use the correct simple past forms of verbs from the box.

arrive	crash	feel	have	sleep
be	fall asleep	get up	leave	wake up

Yesterday morning, I (1) _____ at 5:30 because I (2) _____ a 9:00 A.M. flight to Sydney, Australia. I usually sleep until 8:00 or 9:00, so I (3) _____ not _____ enough last night.

I (4) _____ my house at 6:30 and (5) _____ at the airport two hours before the flight. Everything (6) _____ fine, but I (7) _____ really tired. So after getting on the plane, I immediately (8) _____.

While sleeping, I had a dream that there was a problem on the plane. The plane fell from the sky, and it was going straight toward the ground! But just before the plane (9) _____, I (10) _____. What a terrible dream to have on a plane! At least it didn't crash in real life—I got to Sydney just fine.

ASSIGNMENT

Write about a dream that you had.

PREPARE TO WRITE

A. Discuss the questions with a partner.

1. Think about a recent dream. Were you alone in the dream? Were you with others? Explain.

2. Think about the place in the dream. Were you inside or outside? Was it a familiar place, or was it unknown to you? Describe what you saw.

3. How did you feel in the dream? Happy? Afraid? Nervous? Stressed?

4. Think about the events in the dream. What happened first? What happened in the middle? How did the dream end?

5. How did you feel after you woke up from the dream?

B. Use the timeline to put the events in your dream in order.

WRITE

Write a one-paragraph story of your dream. Start at the beginning, telling about the people and place in the dream. Then tell what happened (the events). Finish with how the dream ended and how you felt. Give your paragraph a title.

_____

_____

_____

_____

_____

_____

_____

_____

PROOFREAD AND EDIT

A. Proofread your story.

- Do you include the people and place(s) in your dream?
- Do you write about the events in your dream?
- Do you have a concluding sentence about your dream's ending?
- Is your story in the form of a paragraph?
- Do you use time signal words?
- Do you use the simple past correctly?
- Are there any spelling mistakes?

B. Work with your partner. Share your stories. Answer the questions in the Peer Review Form. Share feedback. Then edit your story.

Peer Review Form	Yes	No
1. Does your partner write about his or her dream?	☐	☐
2. Does your partner write about the people and places in his or her dream?	☐	☐
3. Does your partner write about the events in his or her dream?	☐	☐
4. Does your partner have a concluding sentence about the dream's ending?	☐	☐
5. Does your partner use time signal words?	☐	☐
6. Does your partner use the simple past correctly?	☐	☐
7. Are there any spelling mistakes? If there are, circle them.	☐	☐

⬆ Go to **MyEnglishLab** to complete grammar and vocabulary practices.

DEVELOP SOFT SKILLS

USING FLASHCARDS TO LEARN NEW VOCABULARY

You will read and hear a lot of new vocabulary in your college classes. You need a good system to study and learn these new words. One good system is using flashcards. Flashcards are a fun and helpful way to study new words and test your memory of them.

A. Read the words and definitions. You will see these words in the text on the next page.

> Glossary
>
> out loud: using your voice so that other people can hear you
>
> part of speech: one of the different types of words, based on how words are used (as nouns or verbs, for example)

B. Read the text.

Studying Vocabulary with Flashcards

chase

The front of a flashcard

Meaning: follow someone or something fast, trying to catch them

Verb

Example: In my dream, a dog _chased_ me.

HELP!

The back of the flashcard

How to Make Flashcards

1 Flashcards are cards with a word or phrase on the front and information about it on the back. Look at the card above.

Word on the front: Writing the vocabulary word in color can help you remember the word. For example, you can use blue for nouns, red for verbs, and green for adjectives.

Meaning: Sometimes the meaning of the word is in your book. Sometimes you will need to look in a dictionary to find the definition. Many words have more than one meaning. Read all the definitions and choose the one you need. Use an English-to-English dictionary.

Part of speech: Remember that some words can have more than one part of speech.

Example: Writing your own sentence can help you understand the word better. You can also use a sentence from your book or dictionary.

Picture: A picture can help you remember the word. You can draw it yourself or find a picture.

How to Study

2 With your flashcards, try following these steps:

1. Read the word on the front of a card out loud.

2. Try to remember its meaning.

3. Then turn the card over to see if you are correct.

3 Another way to study is to read the definition first. If you remember the word, say it out loud. Then turn the card over to see if you are correct. Using flashcards with a classmate is also a good way to study.

(Continued)

When to Get Started and Study

4 When is the best time to make a flashcard? As soon as you know the word is important to remember. What about studying? Plan to study your cards again and again. Do not stop studying when you think you know the words. Just let a few days pass before you review them the next time. Look at one student's study schedule.

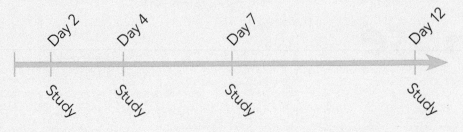

C. Check (✓) all correct answers to each question.

1. What should you write on a flashcard?

☐ your name

☐ a word you want to learn

☐ a definition for the word

☐ the name of your dictionary

☐ the part of speech of the word

☐ an example sentence with the word

CULTURE NOTE

You can also find flashcard apps and flashcard-making programs online. They are a good way to learn vocabulary, too. Hand-made flashcards (using notecards) are nice because they are in your own writing and you can decide exactly what information goes on the back of the card.

2. What are good ways to study and learn your flashcard words?

☐ using color on the cards

☐ drawing pictures on the cards

☐ saying the words out loud

☐ trying to remember the information before turning the card over

☐ practicing with a classmate

☐ reviewing the cards again and again

☐ sleeping with the cards under your pillow

D. Read the questions. Discuss them in a small group.

1. What did you know about flashcards before reading this text?

2. What experiences with flashcards can you describe?

3. Do you think flashcards are helpful for learning new words?

4. What other ideas do you have for how to make and use flashcards? Explain.

E. Choose a word or phrase from the list at the bottom of this page. In the spaces below, make a flashcard. Share your work with a classmate.

Front   Back

WHAT DID YOU LEARN?

Check (✓) the skills and vocabulary you learned. Circle the things you need to practice.

SKILLS

☐ I can understand narratives.

☐ I can write personal stories.

☐ I can use the simple past.

☐ I can understand basic suffixes.

☐ I can use flashcards to learn new vocabulary.

VOCABULARY

☐ afraid

☐ avoid

☐ back at

☐ beginner

☐ bite

☐ brain

☐ busy

☐ chase

☐ climber

☐ create

☐ current

☐ driver

☐ ending

☐ experience

☐ fear

☐ hacker

☐ hole

☐ jungle

☐ live on

☐ meeting

☐ memory

☐ necessary

☐ painting

☐ patient

☐ printer

☐ real life

☐ represent

☐ run away

☐ runner

☐ snake

☐ solve

☐ stay with

☐ strange

☐ stressed

☐ suddenly

☐ trainer

☐ traveler

◐ Go to **MyEnglishLab** to complete a self-assessment.

◐ Go to **MyEnglishLab** for a challenge reading about Psychology.

Index

Photo Credits

Cover: Yuval Helfman/500px/Getty Images.

Design-related images (multi-use): Budai Romeo Gabor/Fotolia(gold coin); Nik_Merkulov/Fotolia(green leaf); Vichly4thai/Fotolia(red molecule DNA); Tobkatrina/123RF(Children Holding Earth); Orelphoto/Fotolia(honeycomb pattern).

Main text: Page v (RW A1 architecture): Vichy Deal/Shutterstock; v (RW A1 genetics): Benjamin Albiach Galan/Shutterstock; v (RW A1 business & technology): Scyther5/123RF; v (RW A1 psychology): Agsandrew/Shutterstock; v (LS A1 architecture): Leonid Andronov/123RF; v (LS A1 genetics): Lightspring/Shutterstock; v (LS A1 business & technology): Scanrail/123RF; v (LS A1 psychology): ESB Professional/Shutterstock; v (RW A2 money & e-commerce): GaudiLab/Shutterstock; v (RW A2 cultural anthropology): Anatoliy_gleb/Shutterstock; v (RW A2 civil engineering): Nito/Shutterstock; v (RW A2 sustainable agriculture): Alexander Raths/Shutterstock; v(LS A2 money & e-commerce): Stanisic Vladimir/Shuttertsock; v (LS A2 cultural anthropology): Suthichai Hantrakul/Shutterstock; v (LS A2 civil engineering): Prochasson Frederic/Shutterstock; v (LS A2 sustainable agriculture): Melhijad/Shutterstock; ix (p. 1 main image): Vichy Deal/Shutterstock; ix (p. 1 thumbnail top): Denis Babenko/Shutterstock; ix(p. 1 thumbnail bottom): Testing/Shutterstock; ix (p. 2): Denis Babenko/Shutterstock; x (p. 5 UAE map): Tupungato/Shutterstock; x (p. 5 Jumeirah Palm Island): Andriy Popov/123RF; xiii (p. 55): Kurhan/Shutterstock; xiv (p. 4 beach): Dashingstock/Shutterstock; xiv (p. 7 The Shard): Cristian Gusa/Shutterstock; xiv (p. 80 seafood): Karel Joseph Noppe Brooks/123RF; xiv (p. 80 dairy): GoncharukMaks/Shutterstock; xiv (p. 80 pizza): Anna Hoychuk/Shutterstock; xiv (p. 80 potatoes): Aberheide/123RF; xiv (p. 80 chicken): Lukas Gojda/Shutterstock; xiv (p. 80 potato chips): Tim UR/Shutterstock; xiv (p. 80 eggs): Vandame/Shutterstock; xiv (p. 80 macaroni & cheese): Kia Cheng Boon/123RF; xiv (p. 80 nuts): Oksana2010/Shutterstock; xiv (p. 80 dumplings): Yevgeniy11/Shutterstock; xv (p. 137): Minerva Studio/Shutterstock; 1 (main image): Vichy Deal/Shutterstock; 1 (thumbnail top): Denis Babenko/Shutterstock; 1 (thumbnail bottom): Testing/Shutterstock; 2: Denis Babenko/Shutterstock; 3 (New York): Luciano Mortula/123RF; 3 (Paris): Iakov Kalinin/123RF; 3 (Egyptian pyramid): Patryk Kosmider/Shutterstock; 3 (Chicago): AindriuH/Shutterstock; 4 (beach): Dashingstock/Shutterstock; 4 (heart-shaped plate): Belchonock/123RF; 5 (UAE map): Tupungato/Shutterstock; 5 (Jumeirah Palm Island): Andriy Popov/123RF; 7 (The Shard): Cristian Gusa/Shutterstock; 7 (bedroom): Evgeny Kanashkin/123RF; 8: Jarun Ontakrai/Shutterstock; 9: Jerry Portelli/Shutterstock; 11 (bottom): Elvetica/Shutterstock; 13: Svetlana Deyneko/Shutterstock; 14: Photographee.eu/Shutterstock; 16 (Map of Hawaii): Kaesler Media/Shutterstock; 16 (Mars): Michael Rosskothen/123RF; 16 (HI-SEAS): Courtesy of HI-SEAS/University of Hawaii at Manoa; 17: Mona Makela/Shutterstock; 18 (HI-SEAS): Courtesy of HI-SEAS/University of Hawaii at Manoa; 19: Svet_Feo/Shutterstock; 21: Nixki/Shutterstock; 22: Photobac/Shutterstock; 24: Testing/Shutterstock; 25 (solar panels): Luiza Klata-Subicka/123RF; 25 (beach): Iofoto/123rf; 26: Jeff Smith - Perspectives/Shutterstock; 27 (beach): Thawatchai Thanapanitsakul/123RF; 27 (Indian Ocean map): Peter Hermes Furian/Shutterstock; 28: Thawatchai Thanapanitsakul/123RF; 29 (birthday): Syda Productions/Shutterstock; 29 (Everest): Daniel Prudek/Shutterstock; 30 (clock): Justdoit777/Shutterstock; 30 (balls): Serezniy/123RF; 30 (computer screen): MishAl/Shutterstock; 30 (glass table): Deusexlupus/123RF; 30 (plastic bottle): Diplikaya/123RF; 30 (metal chair): Michael Kraus/Shutterstock; 30 (wood): Makeitdouble/Shutterstock; 30 (living room): Breadmaker/123RF; 33: Igor Serdiuk/123RF; 34 (left): Galina Peshkova/123RF; 34 (center): Daniela Simona Temneanu/123RF; 34 (right): Dmitry Fisher/Shutterstock; 36: Toniflap/Shutterstock; 37 (1): Konstantin L/Shutterstock; 37 (2): Sean Pavone/Shutterstock; 37 (3): Digitalr/123RF; 37 (4): Pavel Konovalov/123RF; 37 (5): Nikonaft/Shutterstock; 37 (6): Donvictorio/Shutterstock; 37 (7): Taiftin/123RF; 38 (Jumeirah Palm Island): Andriy Popov/123RF; 38 (palm tree): PzAxe/Shutterstock; 39 (top): Betsey Shapiro/Shutterstock; 39 (bottom): Droneandy/Shutterstock; 41 (A): Sborisov/123RF; 41 (B): HelloRF Zcool/Shutterstock; 41 (C): Belikova/123RF; 41 (D): Yelo34/123RF; 47 (main image): Benjamin Albiach Galan/Shutterstock; 47 (thumbnail top): Mark Bowden/123RF; 47 (thumbnail bottom, left): Siegfriedkopp/123RF; 47 (thumbnail bottom, right): Stocksolutions/123RF; 48: Mark Bowden/123RF; 49: Mark Bowden/123RF; 50: Niceregionpics/Shutterstock; 51 (top): Designua/Shutterstock; 51 (bottom): David Orcea/Shutterstock; 52 (straight hair): Bbtreesubmission/123RF; 52 (wavy hair): Gareth Boden/Pearson Education Ltd; 52 (curly hair): Rehan Qureshi/Shutterstock; 53 (women smiling): Jon Barlow/Pearson Education Ltd; 53 (man smiling): Martin Allinger/Shutterstock; 55: Kurhan/Shutterstock; 56: Dean Drobot/123RF; 57: Stockyimages/Shutterstock; 58 (mustache): Shutterstock; 58 (beard): Antonio Sanchez/Shutterstock; 58 (cute): Africa Studio/Shutterstock; 58 (pretty): Sergey Nivens/123RF; 58 (handsome): Daxiao Productions/Shutterstock; 58 (good looking): Imtmphoto/Shutterstock; 59 (man): Kues/Shutterstock; 59 (woman and children): Petro/123RF; 61: Linn Currie/Shutterstock; 65 (two students): KPG_Payless/Shutterstock; 65 (three students): Goodluz/Shutterstock; 68 (left): Siegfriedkopp/123RF; 68 (right): Stocksolutions/123RF; 69 (burger & fries): Elena Shashkina/Shutterstock; 69 (sashimi): Dropu/Shutterstock; 69 (broccoli): Dream79/Shutterstock; 69 (dumplings): Coasehsieh/Shutterstock; 69 (fruit): Siegfriedkopp/Shutterstock; 69 (Korean BBQ): Keiphotostudio/Shutterstock; 69 (blue cheese): Serezniy/123RF; 69 (tacos): Jes Abeita/Shutterstock; 69 (strawberries): EM Arts/Shutterstock; 69 (kale, spinach & broccoli): Decius/123RF; 71 (woman eating pepper): Ocskaymark/123RF; 71 (Indian food): Stocksolutions/123RF; 72 (human tongue): Designua/Shutterstock; 72 (chocolate cake): Alex Kolokythas Photography/Shutterstock; 72 (hot peppers): Lukas Belak/Shutterstock; 73: Margouillat photo/Shutterstock; 74 (Sichuan tofu): Bonchan/Shutterstock; 74 (woman eating pizza): Ivanko80/Shutterstock; 76 (tomatoes): Monika Olszewska/Shutterstock; 76 (cookies & milk): Martellostudio/Shutterstock; 76 (orange juice): Sergei Vinogradov/123RF; 76 (fish): Jacek Chabraszewski/Shutterstock; 76 (sandwich): Badmanproduction/123RF; 76 (potatoes): Shutterstock; 77: Fierman Much/Shutterstock; 78 (dim sum): Leungchopan/Shutterstock; 78 (falafel): Igor Dutina/Shutterstock; 78 (hummus): David Kadlec/123RF; 80 (seafood): Karel Joseph Noppe Brooks/123RF; 80 (dairy): GoncharukMaks/Shutterstock; 80 (pizza): Anna Hoychuk/Shutterstock; 80 (potatoes): Aberheide/123RF; 80 (chicken): Lukas Gojda/Shutterstock; 80 (potato chips): Tim UR/Shutterstock; 80 (eggs): Vandame/Shutterstock; 80 (macaroni & cheese): Kia Cheng Boon/123RF; 80 (nuts): Oksana2010/Shutterstock; 80 (dumplings): Yevgeniy11/Shutterstock; 81: Auremar/123RF; 82 (chili): Vkuslandia/Shutterstock; 82 (young boy eating): Anyka/123RF; 87 (top): Jon Barlow/Pearson Education Ltd; 87 (bottom): Baranq/Shutterstock; 89(main image): Scyther5/Shutterstock; 89 (thumbnail, top): Ronstik/Shutterstock; 89 (thumbnail, bottom): Igor Kardasov/Shutterstock; 90: Ronstik/Shutterstock; 91: Mirko Vitali/Shutterstock; 92: Oleksiy Mark/Shutterstock; 93 (top): Serezniy/123RF; 93 (bottom): MarcelClemens/Shutterstock; 95 (laptop): Oleksandr_Delyk/Shutterstock; 99: Vicenfoto/123RF; 100: Karelnoppe/123RF; 101: Georgejmclittle/Shutterstock; 106 (1): Lzflzf/123RF; 106 (2): Flower travelin' man/Shutterstock; 106 (3): Andrey_Popov/Shutterstock; 106 (4): Andrey_Popov/Shutterstock; 106 (5): Rawpixel.com/Shutterstock; 106 (6): Oleksiy Mark/Shutterstock; 106 (7): Pcruciatti/Shutterstock; 107: Ra2studio/Shutterstock; 108: Sergey Korkin/123RF; 109 (dinner table on cellphone): Jakobradlgruber/123RF; 117: Yuriy Chertok/Shutterstock; 120: Igor Kardasov/Shutterstock; 121 (top, left): Elnur/Shutterstock; 121 (top, center): Elnur Amikishiyev/123RF; 121 (top, right): Elnur/Shutterstock; 121 (bottom, left): Elnur Amikishiyev/123RF; 121 (bottom, right): Elnur/Shutterstock; 124: Magiceyes/Shutterstock; 126: Iakov Filimonov/123RF; 130 (top): Petrnutil/123RF; 130 (bottom): Martin Novak/Shutterstock; 136: Antonio Guillem/Shutterstock; 137: Minerva Studio/Shutterstock; 138: James Weston/Shutterstock; 142: Maryna Riazanska/Shutterstock; 144 (top): Dmitry Melnikov/Shutterstock; 144 (bottom): C.PIPAT/Shutterstock; 145: Leah-Anne Thompson/Shutterstock; 147 (main image): Agsandrew/Shutterstock; 147 (thumbnail top): Blend Images/Shutterstock; 147 (thumbnail bottom): Ljupco/123RF; 148: Blend Images/Shutterstock; 149: Nenad Aksic/Shutterstock; 150: Mark Bowden/123RF; 151: Wavebreakmedia/Shutterstock; 152: Egd/Shutterstock; 157: Paolo Bona/Shutterstock; 160 (basketball): Dotshock/Shutterstock; 160 (soccer): Makieni/Shutterstock; 160 (baseball): Mtaira/123RF; 160 (video games): Bogdan Mircea Hoda/Shutterstock; 160 (guitar): Africa Studio/Shutterstock; 160 (piano): Tomasz Markowski/Shutterstock; 161 (taekwondo): Kzenon/Shutterstock; 161 (yoga): Design Exchange/Shutterstock; 161 (jogging): Jacek Chabraszewski/Shutterstock; 161 (swimming): Wavebreak Media Ltd/123RF; 161 (friends): Pixelheadphoto digitalskillet/Shutterstock; 161 (saxophone): Africa Studio/Shutterstock; 161 (drums): LightField Studios/Shutterstock; 163: Motive56/Shutterstock; 164: Jenwich Benjapong/Shutterstock; 170: Wavebreak Media Ltd/123RF; 172: Wang Tom/123RF; 174: Ljupco/123RF; 175 (women sleeping): Ollyy/Shutterstock; 175 (mosque): Nick Brundle/Shutterstock; 177 (MRI scan): Ian Allenden/123RF; 177 (rabbit): Tsstockphoto/123RF; 178: Morphart Creation/Shutterstock; 179 (man sleeping): Minerva Studio/Shutterstock; 179 (Zeus): IMG Stock Studio/Shutterstock; 182: Wavebreakmedia/Shutterstock; 185 (Freud): AISA - Everett/Shutterstock; 185 (nervous system): Naveen Kalwa/123RF; 188 (runner): Lordn/Shutterstock; 188 (climb): Inu/Shutterstock; 188 (driver): Sirtravelalot/Shutterstock; 188 (travel): Kudla/Shutterstock; 188 (printer): Tankist276/Shutterstock; 188 (ski): Nataliia Zhekova/123RF; 188 (typewriter): Yiorgosgr/123RF; 188 (meeting): Shutterstock; 190 (jungle): Niradj/123RF; 190 (snake): Hairy Azmeer/123RF; 194 (A): Melpomen/123RF; 194 (B): Stokkete/Shutterstock; 194 (C): Vitaliy Kytayko/123RF; 194 (D): Tom Wang/Shutterstock.